Hypnotised

A Journey Through Trance Music

1990 → 2005

The demand for a book on trance music is now greater than ever. Trance, like various other electronic music genres that went through years of popular appeal, imploded in more recent years. Sometimes, global interest seems to return, but the true spirit from its era of origin never really comes back.

As I write this, it has been close to fifteen years since I started losing that connection I had with trance back in the day. However, there is a feeling of nostalgia that made me realise that many of us still tie the same memories and connections to some of the best music from that era. I felt it would be of interest to look back by capturing all information on the genre in a physical object.

Hence, this book ought to offer a wide perspective on trance music and covers material that is most relevant in a personal way. However, it is not meant to be read as a linear, historical narrative of trance music, nor a chronological overview of its evolutions and outcomes.

My intention was to develop a broad and far-reaching

trance encyclopaedia, outlining some of the genre's most prominent artists, labels and releases over the course of fifteen years.

A simple digital publication wouldn't have done the trick. In order to remain relevant for as long as possible, the physical format emerged as an essential aspect of this project.

Arjan Rietveld

HISTORY
→ 18
SUBGENRES
→ 46
DUTCH DIMENSION
→ 66
RELEASES
→ 86
LABELS
→ 258
ALBUMS
→ 320
COLOPHON
→ 332

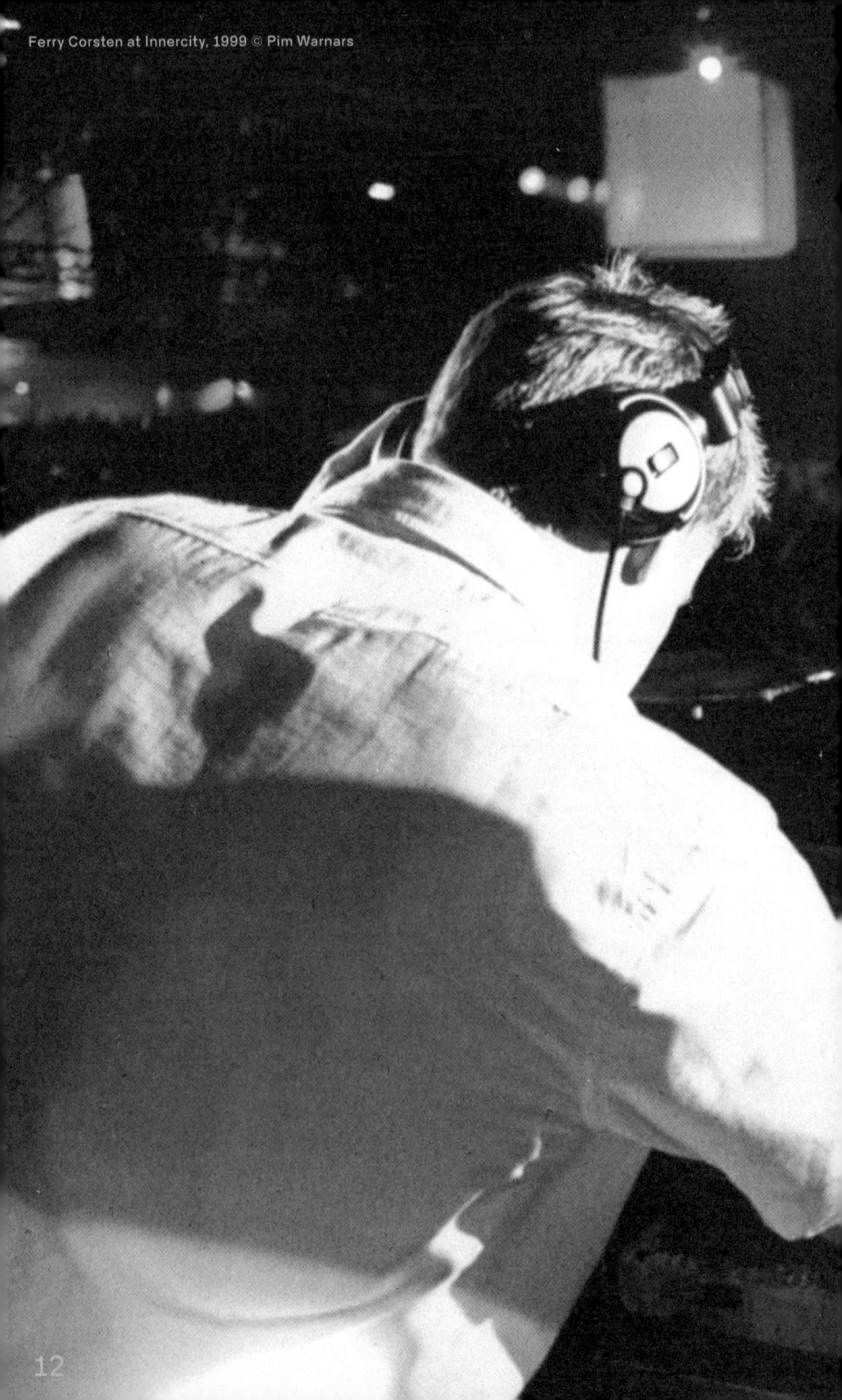
Ferry Corsten at Innercity, 1999 © Pim Warnars

Armin van Buuren at Innercity, 1999 © Pim Warnars

You came in from the darkness and held the door open wide
   You stood there like a vision before my unbelieving eyes
   I believe in what I see and also what I hear
   But did the night play tricks on me or were you really there
   Am I being hypnotised?

HISTORY

CHAPTER 1
TRANCEFORMATION

Trance: the mere word itself triggers off responses as enigmatic as the nature of sound itself. For some, trance equates to a mind-numbing assault of sounds, colours and movement, inextricable from the environment of sound systems and clubs. To others, trance represents a more personal experience—like a soothing tonic of strings and rhythms, as well as a way to articulate the feelings and anxieties of a rapidly changing world.

Under more common usage, trance reflects the earlier and now obsolete concept of 'a dazed, half-conscious or insensible condition or state of fear'—drawing its origin from the Old French word transe (meaning: 'fear of evil') and the Latin verb transire (meaning: 'to cross' or 'pass over'). To sum it up, the term trance denotes any state of awareness or consciousness other than normal waking consciousness, which may occur involuntarily.

Trance conjures up a wealth of states and mindsets, spanning all types of fluctuating emotions, moods and daydreams that human beings may experience. All activities involving human presence organically imply the filtering of information which translate through sensory modalities and this process affects both our brain's functioning and consciousness. Therefore, trance can be understood as an influence for the mind to invert or alter the way it filters information, resulting in making diversified use of the mind's time and resources.

Both a natural and acquired state of being, entered when the physical envelope goes to sleep while the mind stays awake, trance implies crucial changes in the response of brain waves corresponding to changes in levels of mental activity. In other words, the less mental activity going on, the deeper the level of trance one will experience.

Trance-like states may deliberately be triggered via specific techniques and ecstasy-inducing practices such as prayer, religious rituals, meditation, physical exercise, sex, music, dancing, sweating, fasting, thirsting or psychotropic drugs. All can act as different portals to the unconscious for purposes as diverse but complementary as relaxation, healing, intuition and inspiration. Such techniques used by an individual to induce a state of ecstasy are generally associated with their particular religious or cultural background.

To give further historical insight of trance's fundamental nature, many traditions and ancient rituals nurtured and developed their own version of trance. Each version proved to have a distinct range of functions and applications both in the religious and mystical world in general, including that of shamanism and also some elements of Buddhist philosophy.

These interpretations of trance-like states of mind often include statements about contact with supernatural or spiritual beings, revelatory enlightenment, or to a subsequent change of values, attitudes and behaviour, influenced by a religious experience. Traces of such practices can be found the world over since the dawn of time, amongst a liturgy of religions including Christianity, Buddhism, Hinduism and Greek and Roman mythology.

Though often associated with Eastern and Indigenous cultures in modern times, trance was bound to, sooner or later, expand extensively across modern Western civilisation—opening up to a vast horizon of new possibilities for oneself. This newfound state of liberation, dedicated to unshackling 'trancers' from the straitjacket of ordinary reality, or what some call 'the prison of the senses', could help man finally transcend the boundaries of time and space as one has come to know and experience them.

Obviously, a genre that bears the name 'trance' can only draw parallels with the wider and largely entwined web of cultural and religious behaviours aforementioned, making possible all sorts of interconnections between music and the multi-secular traditions that trance—in the broadest sense of the term—can be linked to.

In its earlier stages and impersonations, trance-inducing music attempted to emulate trance-like states themselves, translating the associated feelings of high, chills, euphoria and uplifting rush listeners would experience inwardly in the shape of sound. A first artistic statement was made by German composer Klaus

Schulze, back in the early eighties.

The Berlin School pioneer then concentrated on mixing minimalist music with repetitive rhythmic motifs, arpeggiated sounds, composing several albums of atmospheric space experimentality that would come to be known as kosmische. As the titles suggest, his two albums Trancefer (1981), followed by En=Trance (1987), clearly referred to the induced mindset that his music was aiming to convey.

Amongst the new wave of modern-day electronic music producers to have taken the scene by storm in the late eighties and early nineties. Seminal British act The KLF was the first to make a noted reference to trance on their 1988 track What Time Is Love (Pure Trance 1), which is also annotated on the record sleeve as Pure Trance. Another crucial nod came with German production duo Dance 2 Trance, whose first single came out in 1991, followed by various artists and outfits such as Art Of Trance, Cygnus X and The Visions Of Shiva.

CHAPTER 2
TRAVELOGUE

Let's reel back to summer 1987. A group of British friends travel to the island of Ibiza for a week to celebrate the twenty-fourth birthday of one of theirs—a young chap going by the name of Paul Oakenfold. Along with his friends Nicky Holloway, Danny Rampling and Johnny Walker, Oakenfold discovers a then little-known club called Amnesia and its resident DJ—Alfredo. Instead of taking home the tourist's starter-pack of glorious bronze-ish suntan and blurry holiday snaps to remember the sunny days, the men returned home knackered, but brewing with what could then be called a missionary zeal.

Three of them would soon launch their own club night in London: Paul Oakenfold created Spectrum (with Johnny Walker as a resident DJ), Danny Rampling started Shoom and Nicky Holloway gave birth to The Trip. Within months, the parties' reputation and attractiveness went skyrocketing and Spectrum quickly turned into one of the country's major acid house nights.

Following the developments of electronic music in the United States—notably the New York and Chicago house scenes as well as the rise of Detroit techno in the eighties, another Western-European movement played a notable role in the development of electronic music on the continent. During the late eighties, the sound of new beat originated in Belgium. Being a lower-pitched cross-over between acid house and electronic body music (EBM), the underground subculture associated with new beat was particularly thriving during the 1987-1988 period.

These early movements attributed the first forms and incarnations of trance-engineered music which emerged in the early nineties. By then, house music had already taken hold and techno had also started to gain momentum in Europe. The dance revolution was to rapidly grip the United Kingdom and mainland Europe.

In parallel to the rise of this new musical order, the fall of the Berlin Wall in East-Germany in 1989 made way for cultural tectonic shifts. The capital moved from controlled austerity to a sense of overwhelming hedonism that still persists today and of which electronic music became a catalyst as much as a byproduct.

The open spirit of Berlin and its inhabitants became apparent through its vibrant musical upsurge, along with the rise of key clubs such as E-Werk (hosted in an electric substation since 1993) and Tresor (formed in the vaults of a former department store in 1991, as a substitute to the Ufo Club that closed in 1990), pushing especially house and techno music—all quickly becoming praised bastions for free-minded raving.

A haven for ravers as much as an unmatched hub for creativity, Berlin brought the likes of Cosmic

Baby, Kid Paul and Paul van Dyk to the forefront. The city's movement became apparent on a more global level through the Love Parade, a large-scale street march celebrating diversity, born in July 1989. Initially a political demonstration for peace and international understanding through love and music, its first gathering took 150 people to the streets in Berlin. The Love Parade turned into an annual event and in subsequent years grew to over one million participants, until its dramatic ending in Duisburg in 2010.

Right at the intersection of the Belgian and East-German movements, Frankfurt developed itself as a hotbed for early trance and techno music, as music venues such as Dorian Gray (located inside Frankfurt Airport since 1978), Omen (opened in 1988) and Technoclub (founded in 1984) morphed into Europe's largest and most influential nightclubs of their time. Additionally, the sound of Frankfurt came to define itself through the output of labels such as Eye Q, FAX +49-69/450464, Force Inc., Harthouse and Superstition soon became into trend-setting and influential institutions within the boundaries of electronic music.

A crucially important name in the development of the local scene in Frankfurt is Sven Väth. Being involved with club life since the early eighties, Väth became heavily influenced by the sounds he experienced during his extended trips to Goa at the time. Back in his hometown, he became a resident DJ at Dorian Gray, co-founded Omen and launched the Eye

Q imprint together with Heinz Roth and Matthias Hoffman in 1991, followed by the Harthouse label the year after. After ceasing to operate both labels in 1997, resulting in their definitive closure in 1998, Väth instead focused his energy on the Cocoon event series, set up in Ibiza in 1996 and soon developed its fabled twin label imprint at the turn of the millennium.

CHAPTER 3
STRANGE WORLD

Electronic music and nightlife are two notions that seem to go organically hand in hand and venues around the world have played an elemental role in facilitating electronic music since the seventies. By the end of the eighties, early forms of trance were pushed in specific club scenes—most notably in the cities of Berlin, Frankfurt and London, as well as the island of Ibiza. These scenes subsequently turned out to be highly influential for the development of the genre as a whole.

The fact that electronic music proved to be a particularly efficient and meaningful way to let off the weekly stresses of life with friends on the weekend helped forge the genre's identity. Clubs have been and remain—if not a new kind of church—the crucial link between the emitter of music and its receiver: the crowd, including dancers, dreamers and seekers of distraction from the daily struggles of life—those looking to elevate through the sharing of their common love for music. It is all about giving in to the sound, getting locked in motion and in to a trance-like state of mind in which time and space are no longer a thing.

Meanwhile, the consumption of ecstasy amongst other hallucinogenic drugs had gained common ground within global nightlife culture. The synthetic substance was initially used to improve psychotherapy in the seventies, but soon became a popular recreational drug in the eighties, inducing the kind of effects sought by dancers and ravers such as increased empathy, euphoria and heightened sensations. With the trance sound aiming to trigger off such emotions altogether, the optimal effects induced by the joint action of ecstasy, trance music and lighting, logically resulted in the development of ecstasy as the drug of choice for this generation of clubbers.

Around the mid-nineties, the United Kingdom became the epicentre of the new trance phenomenon, taking the sound to new heights in clubs and out to the clubbers' paradise that is Ibiza. DJs such as Dave Seaman, John Digweed, Nick Warren, Paul Oakenfold and Sasha started to open the ears of the clubbing population to whole new perspectives. They were able to put together long-stretched, winding narratives by building up club nights in a deep, precise and emotional manner, inevitably leading to a new form of the so-called progressive sound—incorporating genres such as breakbeat, house and techno.

DJing itself became more of an art form by defining track selection and mixing skills as stand-out characteristics. These traits were made further palpable by the popularity of the mix-CD format, on which reconstructions of such stories would be pressed. In-demand mix series such as Global Underground, Ministry Of Sound and Renaissance played a decisive role in making the 'late' progressive sound of these artists available to a more diverse and global audience—for better or worse.

Also, large-scale clubs such as Cream (opened in 1992), Gatecrasher (founded in 1993) and the Godskitchen events series rapidly showed themselves eager to cater the sound domestically. Hosting thousands of clubbers at a time, their all-night events became synonymous with the trance sound of the time and were quickly accompanied by outdoor festivals set up by those same clubs—including Creamfields, Gatecrasher and Homelands.

The island of Ibiza, an autonomous region of Spain best known for its association with nightlife and hippie gatherings since the sixties, played an equally important role in exploiting a once underground scene. Superclubs such as Amnesia, Eden, Es Paradis, Ku and Space projected the largest trance programs during their opening seasons. When played in the lavish settings of Ibiza, winding tracks with monumental breakdowns, strong melodic hooks and uplifting lead lines—think Café Del Mar by German duo Energy 52, For An Angel by Paul van Dyk and Seven Cities by Solarstone—scored a direct hit in the hearts of an audience looking for new energy and excitement.

Trance music soon established itself as a major force in the European club circuit. The Netherlands picked up a leading role in developing large-scale trance events such as Dance Valley, Mysteryland and Sensation across the country—before exploiting some of these concepts globally. Securing prime-time spots in these events from an early stage on, the foundation was set to a new order that would soon see Dutch artists such as Armin van Buuren, DJ Tiësto and Ferry Corsten turn into some of the most in-demand DJs. Henceforth, it didn't take long until the American and Eastern European markets absorbed the trance sound that once seemed to be a frenetic European affair only.

CHAPTER 4
TRANZY STATE OF MIND

By the turn of the century, the media began to really pick up on the growth and increasingly important place taken by electronic music and club culture in the life of the younger generation. Even traditional media sources boosted the hype around trance music: artist features were to be found in newspapers and magazines, while music tracks and videos were broadcast on a wide range of public radio and television channels.

Radio shows proved to play a major role in bringing the superclubs and DJs straight home to the listeners. The weekly Essential Mix on British channel BBC Radio One—set up by Eddie Gordon and hosted by Pete Tong since its inception in 1993—turned into a hallmark, featuring exclusive guest mixes from electronic music's biggest names. Later on, artist shows such as Armin van Buuren's A State Of Trance series (established in 2001) became heavily influential through broadcasting its weekly shows via multiple domestic radio channels simultaneously—reaching millions of listeners across the globe.

The commercial success of independent labels didn't pass unnoticed with the major music publishers. As a response, various majors set up trance-dedicated sub-branches which made use of their competitive advantage to penetrate the market, in order to reap maximum benefits from the continuously growing market that trance then represented.

Majors such as EMI (with its Additive and Positive branches), Mercury (with Manifesto) and Ministry Of Sound (with Data) were able to capitalise on electronic music by pushing more mainstream sounding acts to the fore. For instance, dance acts such as Fragma, Ian Van Dahl and Lasgo were all featured on the popular British TV program Top Of The Pops.

Meanwhile, the technological development and mass-usage of the internet across the Northern hemisphere, from the turn of the millennium onward, had major implications for the music industry, introducing new ways of thinking in the process. Music became a more widely accessible product, with an even more decisive impact upon those dwelling outside the major cities—who had to this point always been depending on their local music dealer to quench their thirst for new music prior to the emergence of this almighty new digital deity.

With the competition between actors raging, the digital shift of paradigm that came with the new millennium created new challenges for independent labels. Various labels vanished into thin air, or magically resurfaced only years later. In some cases, labels were simply not able to cope with the sudden upsurge of illegal downloads from websites such as LimeWire, Napster and Soulseek—and its negative impact on physical sales. Bankruptcy seemed to be an unavoidable fate for many then, yet somehow other labels managed to withstand the test of time by becoming more flexible and adapting their policies to this intricate new reality.

Those artists, promoters and record labels that did manage to adopt the newfangled possibilities offered by the online world at an early stage, were able to benefit from their pathfinders' status by scaling to a seemingly infinite market potential. The concept of the global superstar DJ accelerated—resulting in a total reinvention of the disc jockey's role and status.

The availability of music production software—another important technological development around the turn of the millennium—made the art of production widely accessible. Back in the day, one needed a fully equipped studio setup as well as a certain technical hardware know-how to produce electronic music, making it both a costly and highly time-consuming exercise. In this new age of computer-aided creation, all that one needed to make beats was a computer with enough storage space to get started and the inspiration to fill it with.

From then on, a new type of music-maker emerged to establish itself as the new standard: the now fabled 'bedroom producer'—a term that's come to encompass nearly all electronic musicians these days. This resulted in a sharp peak in the amount of electronic music produced, inaugurating a new era that would completely redefine the global understanding of dance music and electronic production.

Picking up the scent of a revolution in the making, many labels found themselves eager to surf the wave—pushing monthly and soon weekly releases to consumers the world over. As much as technological innovation was inarguably a blessing for the electronic music scene, its seemingly infinite possibilities ended up being one of several obstacles for the genre's development over time.

As trance's formula was relatively easy to replicate—essentially being built on a four-to-the-floor rhythm and extended with patterns of melody, harmony and repetition—the number of trance records soared constantly. The market was soon saturated with average productions, generally lacking creativity, technological depth, enthusiasm and musical savoir-faire. Quality control and curation were no longer necessary in the thriving online market, where—as a consequence—little to no reference to the roots and true aspirations of early trance were to be found anymore.

CHAPTER 5
THE LEGACY

The successes met by trance have been synonymous with periods of extensive popular appeal, prior to falling victim to the hype bubble it had been building full-bore until it popped. The very markets it once was part of soon became bastions for unlike-minded players more interested in fast-flowing commercial benefits than musical adventurism.

Amongst the elements that have helped fill the space between early trance music and genres more widely broadcast on popular radio stations at that time, vocals played a pivotal role in the massification of trance. Rather low-key from the start, vocals made their way into trance around the turn of the millennium. When trance eventually reached mass popularity, the addition of vocals within instrumental compositions enabled marketers to make trance more accessible to a broader, pop-friendly audience.

Many 12" single releases with a 'hit' potential went on to feature a vocal version in addition to the instrumental. Consequently, of the small cluster of tracks that eventually gained FM radio airplay or got the music video treatment, most included vocals.

Delerium's Silence was one of the flagship tunes of trance music to go gangbusters in commercial realms. Featuring vocals by Sarah McLachlan, Silence—which was essentially a pop song—became such a huge success mainly because of the various remixes it got from trance-affiliated artists and more specifically, DJ Tiësto's In Search Of Sunrise remix.

In parallel to an unhealthy number of average productions, other fine examples include Skydive by Freefall featuring Jan Johnston, Beautiful Things by Andain featuring Mavie Marcos, Rapture by Iio featuring Nadia Ali, Hypnotised by Paul Oakenfold featuring Tiff Lacey and Clear Blue Water by OceanLab featuring Justine Suissa.

As the trance sound made it further into the mainstream arena, many of its original fans felt alienated by the capitalisation of their passion. Larger record labels began to cater their sound so that it bridged the gap with pop music, making the sound more appealing to the layman's ear and, following that inversely proportional curve, increasingly strange to the true underground head.

Logically, with such a diverse range of music to harness under the banner of a single genre, it was inevitable for trance to fall victim to its own success. Historic trance figures like Paul van Dyk publicly denounced the path taken by the genre, slating it multiple times as old hat and artistically outdated.

As a result, some of the genre's founding fathers chose to follow more alternative pathways. Paul Oakenfold, for instance, went on to work with Shifty Shellshock from the rap/rock band Crazy Town, DJ Tiësto remixed acts such as Dave Matthews Band,

Madonna and Moby before making a niche for himself in the world of EDM, Armin van Buuren collaborated with Dutch band Krezip and Ferry Corsten's productions returned to more of an electro vein.

CHAPTER 6
TILL WE MEET AGAIN

Though trance music departed the electronic music scene's centre stage, the genre never completely vanished. Quite the contrary, the genre maintained one of the most loyal fanbases in dance music throughout the years and its move back to a more low-key status resulted in the flourishing of many scenes across the world.

For many, trance feels like a universal family, connected and fostered by the special relationship between artists and fans. The sound's trademark optimistic, euphoric and enthusiastic aspects are hard to compete with for any genre out there. Merging the most hectic melodies, stories and narratives, the feels-ridden journey of trance is second to none when it comes to triggering off visions and emotions.

Yet, trance's positive state of mind also made it an easy target for critics and didn't fail to split its own audience in the process. Whichever route it may follow, trance should be feted for the second wind it gave to dance music. For many early fans of trance music who have grown up to the sound of it in the mid-nineties, this was ultimately about steering the genre they love back to its original design: music for the mind, not music for the masses.

Trance music and its key players undoubtedly had a significant influence on future electronic music genres to come, such as electro house and EDM—an abbreviation of the term 'electronic dance music', as well as a complete misuse of its actual meaning. Also, crossovers with genres as diverse as indie rock, pop and soul have become widespread and the genre keeps on interacting and interbreeding with other styles continuously. Its distinctive tonal and melodic tropes have found their way into dubstep, grime, hip-hop and far more into techno and experimental music than purists would ever dare to admit.

Meanwhile, trance keeps reinventing the rules and standards of its own universe—whether it is the commercial variety, the softer kind blurring the lines between trance and melodic techno—such as that of German brainchilds Kompakt and Get Physical, or the Goa-originated sound of psy-trance, which may be the largest and longest—standing underground scene in the world. Shut off from the zeitgeist's fluctuations, these scenes do not appear keen to mix in ideas from the outside, even though within the ecosystem of electronic music there is no way one could ignore the strange, tangled appeal of trance and its offshoots.

DJ Tiësto at Fast Forward Dance Parade, 1999 © Pim Warnars

Ferry Corsten at Fast Forward Dance Parade, 1999 © Pim Wasmars

SUBGENRES

Trance's ability to provoke heavy emotional states, from deep sadness to ecstatic happiness and everything in between, has drawn comparisons with the powerfulness of classical music, relying on recurring motifs such as love, life and dreams, but also more 'concrete' and 'physical' concepts such as nature, parties and technology.

With its quintessential productions employing a 'four-to-the-floor' time signature, tempos up to one hundred and fifty beats per minute and thirty-two beat phrases, trance made wise use of melody, harmony and repetition to create otherworldly, sense-awakening experiences.

Before turning into its own full-blown style, emancipated from its sometimes complicated lineage with techno and house music, trance happened to be more of a volatile poetic element, finding its way across a wealth of genres and not just a single category of sounds.

At the start of the nineties, most of the electronic music being produced was based on samples. Sampling technology was relatively new at the time and had become affordable enough for it to become a mainstream tool for production.

Early forms of trance were characterised by a minimum use of percussion, a strong emphasis on repetitive melodic chords and arpeggios. The sound was also commonly labelled as techno-trance, as the distinction between the formerly introduced techno sound and the newly developed (and non-existent) trance sound was rather vague and yet to be born as such.

By the middle of the decade, however, pioneers were looking to take their sound in a new direction. This led to the resurgence of the lovelorn synthesizer which, despite being heavily used in the early eighties, had been rather overlooked since the sample-based electronic music revolution of the mid-eighties.

Opening new pathways for electronic-borne aesthetics and subsequently putting on offer a new understanding for its means of production, trance emphasised brief synthesizer lines repeated endlessly throughout tracks, with only the addition of minimal rhythmic changes and occasional synthesizer soundscapes to distinguish them.

Extra percussive elements were usually blended in and major transitions, builds or climaxes regularly find themselves foreshadowed by lengthy snare rolls—quick succession of snare drum hits that build in velocity, frequency and volume towards the end of a measure or phrase. Also, mid-song breakdowns would leave the melody, atmospherics, or both, to stand alone for anywhere from a few seconds to minutes.

Across the second half of the nineties, as trance music grew to a dominating position in clubs and continued to do commercially well into the first decade of the new millennium, most of the trance music featured in the charts strayed away from the actual sound that was then being played in underground trance clubs. As a consequence, the genre went on to split into distinct derivatives, each of which began to develop their own rules, tropes and market.

The following subgenres are identified as a means to denote the differences in sound and aesthetic. Nevertheless, as labelling material could also interfere with the listening experience, the releases featured in this book are arranged alphabetically.

ACID TRANCE

Emerging in the late eighties and early nineties and also known as the 'first wave' of trance, acid trance may be considered a descendant of the acid house movement since the trance genre itself had not yet been invented. The trademark sound of acid is produced with a Roland TB-303 bass machine, by playing a sequenced melody while altering the instrument's filter cut-off frequency, resonance, envelope modulation and accent controls. This real-time tone adjustment was not part of the instrument's original intended operation.

The roots of acid trance are spread across Germany and the United Kingdom, where preceding genres such as acid house and techno already played a notable role in local clubs and labels including Harthouse, Important and No Respect spread the acid-infused sound. Notable artists include Balil, Cosmic Baby, Cygnus X, Hardfloor, Earth Nation, Formic Acid, Oliver Lieb, Resistance D, RMB and Union Jack.

AMBIENT TRANCE

Putting emphasis on tone and atmosphere over traditional musical structure or rhythm to evoke an atmospheric, visual or unobtrusive quality. Ambient music originated in the United Kingdom in the seventies, when new sound-making devices such as the synthesizer were being introduced to a wider market. Balancing the sound of ambient and early trance records, ambient house occurred as a response to the popular harder releases in the early nineties. The sound perfectly suited the newborn electronic home-listening experience, while also being played at chill-out rooms in clubs. Labels such as Mille Plateaux, Planet Dog and Warp were some of the first to facilitate these more experimental sound forms.

Meanwhile, Pete Namlook and his FAX +49-69/450464 imprint dived into the spacier realms of ambient music. Following the directions of his platform and its sublabels, Namlook paved the way for ambient trance productions and remixes—which was gladly taken up by producers such as Michael Woods. Covering both fields, notable artists include 4Voice, Aphex Twin, Banco De Gaia, Boards Of Canada, GAS, Moby, Orbital, Tetsu Inoue, The KLF and The Orb.

ANTHEM TRANCE

When the sound of trance became more popular in the late nineties, being 'consumed' across many parts of the world, most of the groundbreaking German trance labels from the early nineties moved to the background, preceded by more commercially viable platforms. Meanwhile, major labels started to set up their own trance divisions. Musically speaking and following the creation of the Roland JP-8000 and Access Virus synthesizers, 'super-saw' sounds took a more prominent part in releases. Anthem-like sounds became widely associated with tides of emotional submersion and their capacity at generating an epic feel, though being much lighter in tone.

Also, artists began to attract more of the light on them and new marketing ways and technological developments around the late nineties helped newly established labels dominate the global market. Vocals also started to play a more notable role in productions. Name variations of this more popularised form of trance include commercial trance, epic trance and uplifting trance, whilst the term is also widely confused with euro dance (or, worse, euro trance). Notable artists include Agnelli & Nelson, Binary Finary, Blank & Jones, Gareth Emery, Gouryella, Matt Darey, Minimalistix, Paul van Dyk, Push and Rank 1.

BALEARIC TRANCE

Following the emergence of Balearic beat in the early nineties, a more soothing vein found its way into trance as a counterpoint to the harder-hitting, anthemic sound that became more firmly established within the Northern European club scenes. Capturing the mood of a soft, Mediterranean sunset perfectly, Balearic trance generally featured a mix of string instruments, like Spanish guitars and mandolins, combined with diverse sonic tropes commonly associated with Mediterranean seascapes, such as the ocean and birds.

Laying further emphasis on the atmosphere through the layering of stretched-out, spacious pads, Balearic trance bears a close resemblance to—and borrowed elements from—the earlier ambient trance movement. Originally named after the Balearic island of Ibiza, the genre is often also referred to as Ibiza trance. By the end of the nineties, an array of labels including Lost Language, Massive Drive and Xtravaganza managed to capitalise on Balearic trance's then-nascent global appeal, soon translating it to wider international recognition. Notable artists include ATB, Chicane, Energy 52, Humate, Jam & Spoon, Nalin & Kane, Salt Tank, Solarstone, Three Drives and York.

DREAM TRANCE

Dream trance experienced a massive upsurge in Italy during the mid-nineties, at the very moment trance broke through to mainstream recognition in Western Europe. The key element of dream trance resides in catchy and 'dreamy' melodies, typically played on an acoustic instrument. The creation of dream trance came as a response to social pressures in Italy during the mid-nineties. The popularity of rave culture and the ensuing popularity of nightclub attendance that grew amongst young adults then resulted in a sad trend of weekly deaths due to car accidents ('strage del sabato sera', or 'Saturday night slaughter'), as clubbers would drive across the country overnight and fall asleep at the wheel, from either strenuous dancing or alcohol and drug abuse.

As a response to the avalanche of fatalities, DJs such as Robert Miles went on to play slower, calming music to conclude their sets, as a means to counteract the effects of the fast-paced, repetitive tracks that preceded, finding a positive echo in the authorities and parents of car crash victims. Italian labels such as DBX, Out and Subway were the first to boost market appeal for dream trance. Notable artists include B.B.E., Daniele Gas, DJ Dado, Lello B., Nylon Moon, Robert Miles, Roland Brant, The Cynic Project, W.P. Alex Remark and Zhi-Vago.

HARD TRANCE

Originating in Frankfurt in the early nineties, hard trance was part of the breakbeat hardcore community that began to fragment into different styles. Hard trance is characterised by strong, hard or even pitched-down kicks, fully resonant basses and an increased amount of reverberation applied to the main beat. The popularity of hard trance initially went with a bang in Germany from the early nineties until the late nineties, with labels such as Frankfurt Beat Productions, Noom and Suck Me Plasma pushing the genre to the fore. Belgian label Bonzai also played a significant role in spreading this harder sound across the globe.

Around the turn of the millennium, when the German sound lost a bit of its traction, the movement began to gain ground in the United Kingdom. Hard trance prefigured the development of the hardhouse movement, soon reaching mass audiences in the United Kingdom with the help of labels such as Nukleuz, Tidy Trax and Vicious Circle. The crowd's interest in hard trance soon faded to the advantage of newer forms of trance music, especially tech-trance. Notable artists include Alphazone, Commander Tom, DJ Scot Project, DuMonde, Kai Tracid, Sunbeam, The Essence Of Nature, Yakooza, Yoji Biomehanika and Yves Deruyter.

NEO-TRANCE

Neo-trance was one of the latest subdivisions to make it in the genre's distinct vernacular, embodying recent developments towards a more minimalist type of trance. Having its roots in minimal and techno music from Germany, Scandinavia and the United Kingdom, the associated producers incorporated melodic elements and breakdowns from the said styles in order to add further depth and atmosphere to their tracks. Funnily enough, most of these artists were unrelated to, nor interested in the then-popular trance music movement making waves the world over.

Most neo-trance productions are characterised by their radically slower tempo and use of a distinctively more monotonous and limited palette of sounds and elements. Key labels attached to the genre were Border Community, Kompakt and Traum Schallplaten. Notable artists include Âme, Aril Brikha, Booka Shade, Dominik Eulberg, Gui Boratto, James Holden, Kaito, Nathan Fake, The Field and Trentemøller.

PROGRESSIVE TRANCE

Interpreted as another reaction against commercial trance music, the rise of the 'late' progressive sound occurred simultaneously with the development of hard trance. Progressive trance, however, focused on slowing down rather than cranking up the BPMs. Born from the fusion of deep house with basic trance elements such as arpeggios, gated synths, delays and heavy reverb, progressive trance built around more subtle, minor key melodies. Stripped back of its squelchy acidic sounds, anthemic choruses, crescendos and bass chord shifts, the presence of a repeating lead synthesizer sound as well as regular addition and subtraction of layers of sound enhanced a feeling of smooth progression.

The emergence of the genre itself can be traced back to Italy around the mid-nineties, but the sound really found its pace in the United Kingdom, where labels such as Hooj Choons, Renaissance and Silver Planet stepped in and paved the way for new varieties, blending in trance-like patterns with various other genres such as deep house and breakbeat. Also commonly described as progressive house, it became the sound of the world's dance floors by the end of the millennium. Notable artists include Breeder, DJ Remy, Fade, Gigi D'Agostino, Hybrid, Quivver, Salt Tank, Sander Kleinenberg, Sasha and Tilt.

PSYCHEDELIC TRANCE

As trance music put down roots in Europe, the genre also gathered a following in the Indian state of Goa, which had been a popular destination for psychedelic music enthusiasts since the late sixties. Initially intended to assist dancers in experiencing a collective state of bodily transcendence—similar to that of ancient shamanic dancing rituals, through hypnotic, pulsing melodies and rhythms, DJs in Goa had moved from playing psychedelic rock towards more electronic styles during the eighties. Early trance music happened to fit the hypnotic, hallucinogenic Goa scene perfectly. As such, Goa trance established itself during the nineties, being revved-up, energetic and full of spontaneous elements and samples.

While trance was becoming a more commercial affair in Europe, Goa trance evolved into a darker, faster, more progressive style, which was to be baptised psychedelic trance, or psy-trance. Many miles away from Goa, Israel rapidly grew as a safe haven for psy-trance, while British and German labels such as Dragonfly, Gaia Tonträger and Perfecto quickly absorbed the sound as part of their concepts. This was the beginning of cross-continental success for psy-trance, which kept gathering a significant international audience over the years. Notable artists include Astral Projection, Blue Planet Corporation, Hallucinogen, Infected Mushroom, Man With No Name, Mystica, Paul Oakenfold, Sandman, Space Tribe, and Yahel.

TECH-TRANCE

After the commercial climax of trance music a few years into the new millennium, the most widespread variant within trance music was tech-trance. As developed by Dutch and British producers, the origins of tech-trance can be found in the hard trance and techno scenes of the mid-nineties, with pioneer Oliver Lieb counting amongst the genre's driving forces from the early days on.

Defining features of tech-trance are complex electronic rhythms driven by a loud kick drum and percussion, filtered or slightly distorted hi-hat sounds and claps, heavily synthesised sounds and a minimal use of the pads. Creative use of reverb and prominent side-chaining have also been characteristics pioneered by the genre and were embraced and pushed forward by prominent labels such as Anjunabeats, ID&T and Spinnin'. Notable artists include Above & Beyond, John Askew, Joop, Marco V, Marcel Woods, Mauro Picotto, Mojado, Ricky Fobis, Sander van Doorn and Simon Patterson.

Ferry Corsten, DJ Tiësto and Armin van Buuren, 1999

DUTCH DIMENSION

Although trance has not been a Dutch affair since its initiation, the country most definitely occupied a singular position on the exchequer around the turn of the millennium. For many, the Dutch region became synonymous with all things trance. Not only because of its popular music festivals, but most importantly thanks to the multitude of artists who've come to dominate international charts and stages over the years.

Three Dutchmen played a decisive part in this process: Armin van Buuren, Ferry Corsten and Tijs Verwest. Interestingly, this trio shares a common background and evolution, as they all grew up relatively close to each other in the Southern region of the Netherlands, while sharing a deep and lasting interest in music from an early age.

They didn't wait for the new millennium to start working together. Since then, their careers followed a relatively similar course—from years of performances at local venues and non-stop studio grind, to the release of a breakthrough track, onto pushing forward on that momentum to achieve international acclaim.

Each of these artists' initial success was quickly followed by a series of singles, compilation appearances, remixes and their own mix compilations. Meanwhile, events company ID&T secured them prime-time spots on large-scale events such as Innercity, Sensation and Trance Energy.

Another common trait is that they've come to run

privately owned record labels, hence creating expansive networks within and outside the country. This provided them unparalleled opportunities for trance to develop into the tsunami it was bound to become, as well as trusting a powerful position within the ever increasingly global market of electronic music.

As the names of Dutch artists soon became synonymous with high-quality studio output (often labelled as euphoric, fast and melodic), these tight-knit connections paved the way for the Dutch wave of trance to grow unhindered, bringing artists such as Matthew Dekay, Rank 1 and Sander Kleinenberg to the fore of a scene that was still in the process of defining itself. Even to this day, Dutch electronic music acts manage to capture the imagination of party-goers across the globe.

ARMIN VAN BUUREN
25 December 1976, Leiden, Netherlands

Aliases
Amsterdance, Armania, Darkstar, El Guitaro, Gig, Gimmick, Hyperdrive Inc., Misteri A, Perpetuous Dreamer, Problem Boy, Rising Star, The Shoeshine Factory

In groups
Alibi, Armin & Friends, DJ's United, E=mc², Electrix, Gaia, Lilmotion, Major League, Monsieur Basculant, Red & White, Technology, Triple A, Wodka Wasters

Private record label
Armada Music

Raised by a father who was an avid record collector, it goes without saying Armin van Buuren grew a natural interest in music. When a close friend first introduced him into the world of electronic music, Dutch radio DJ and remixer Ben Liebrand soon became Van Buuren's early role model.

This encounter rapidly led Van Buuren to investigate the roots of the electronic music he was then growing fond of and it wasn't long before he got to lay his hands on releases by Jean Michel Jarre and Klaus Schulze. The following and most crucial step for him would be the acquisition of a computer and turntables, finally enabling him to elaborate his own music, now an absolute obsession and life priority.

In 1995, in parallel to his studies at Leiden University, Van Buuren began his DJ career at club Nexus in Leiden—the place where he learnt the ropes of extended jockeying in playing six to seven-hour DJ sets on a regular basis. During school holidays, Van Buuren used to play more than four times a week. Another crucial step was taken in 1999 when Van Buuren met Dave Lewis, who helped him break through as a DJ in both the United Kingdom and the United States.

That same year, Van Buuren gladly saw some of his demos land on various compilations and when the first cheques came in, all of the money was instantly invested back into gear for his production studio. Note, Van Buuren was only nineteen years old when his first hit, Blue Fear, was released on Cyber Records in 1995.

It took Van Buuren four years to follow up to this success with his next Cyber Records single, Communication. The track went on to become a major hit on the island of Ibiza in 1999. In the same year, Van Buuren kicked off his own record label, Armind, in collaboration with United Recordings.

Out of various studio sessions with DJ Tiësto, two new projects were born: Wonder Where You Are? as Major League (released on Black Hole Recordings) and Eternity as Alibi (issued via Armind). After being licensed to Paul van Dyk's Vandit Records, Eternity became a global chart-topper and instant classic. Another key tune in Van Buuren's career, Exhale, made in collaboration with Ferry Corsten, soon followed.

Amongst other notable productions, worth quoting are The Sound Of Goodbye as Perpetuous Dreamer, Touch Me as Rising Star and 4 Elements as Gaia (with Benno de Goeij), plus remixes for Moogwai's Viola, Aria's Dido and Yahel's Devotion. Van Buuren released his debut album 76 in 2003.

FERRY CORSTEN
4 December 1973, Rotterdam, Netherlands

Aliases

4x4, A Jolly Good Fellow, Albion, Bypass, Cyber F, Dance Therapy, Delaquente, Digital Control, DJ Sno-White, DotNL, East West, Eon, Exiter, Farinha, Ferr, Festen, Firmly Undaground, Free Inside, Funk Einsatz, Kinky Toys, Lunalife, Moonman, Party Cruiser, Pulp Victim, Pulse, Raya Shaku, Sidewinder, Skywalker, System F, The Nutter, Zenithal

In groups

2HD, A.N.Y., Alter Native, Blade Racer, Block, Boogie Box, Cada, Discodroids, Double Dutch, Elektrika, Embrace, Energiya, FB, Fernick, G-Freak, Gouryella, LoCo, Mind To Mind, New World Punx, Nixieland, Penetrator, Project Aurora, Riptide, Roef, S.O.A., Scum, Selected Worx, Sons Of Aliens, Soundcheck, Spirit Of Adventure, Starparty, The Tellurians, Veracocha, Vimana

Private record label
Tsunami Records

Back in his teens, Ferry Corsten began saving up the money he would make by washing cars and selling mixtapes to kids in his neighbourhood so he could fund his first keyboard. Though he produced and remixed artists under a flurry of aliases right from the drop of his first record at the tender age of sixteen, Corsten officially deployed his wings as a solo artist one year later. If his first records were mostly leaning towards hardcore and gabber, his following pieces quickly established his name in the club-house and trance music scenes.

Aside from his production work, Corsten started to perform on stage and won his first significant award, De Grote Prijs van Nederland, in 1995. His first single to have made it in the charts, Don't Be Afraid, recorded under the alias of Moonman, would prove to be the launchpad to Corsten's career as a composer. The release of Don't Be Afraid was quickly followed by another big hit, Galaxia.

In 1997, Corsten and his business partner Robert Smit set up Tsunami—a new label created under the patronage of Dutch record company Purple Eye Entertainment. Prior to its release, the promo of his soon-to-be career-changing single Out Of The Blue—this time under the moniker of System F—gained the most durable momentum before eventually hitting the streets.

In 1999 and 2000, Corsten joined forces with DJ Tiësto on a popular new side-project named Gouryella. Although the pair only released four singles, the project became a hallmark for the powerful and melodic Dutch trance sound. Apart from Gouryella, the two also produced music as Vimana, releasing the single We Came on Black Hole Recordings in 1999. Other notable productions from that era include Air as Albion, Pocket Damage as Eon and Carte Blanche as Veracocha (with Vincent de Moor).

Corsten gained notable credits for his remixes of William Orbit's variations of two classical giants: Samuel Barber's Adagio For Strings and Maurice Ravel's Pavane Pour Une Infante Défunte. Soon after, Corsten's first releases under his real name landed, amongst which the most notable single, Punk—revealing the more electro-friendly side of his production.

TIJS VERWEST
17 January 1969, Breda, Netherlands

Aliases
Da Joker, DJ Limited, DJ Tiësto, Drumfire, Handover Circuit, Loop Control, Passenger, Roberto Scilatti, Roze, Stray Dog, Tom Ace, TST, Wild Bunch

In groups
A3, Alibi, Allure, Andante, Banyan Tree, Boys Will Be Boys, Clear View, Clouded Leopard, Conil, Control Freaks, D'Alt Vila, Dokmai, Es Vedrá, Flowerchild, Glycerine, Gouryella, Hammock Brothers, Hard Target, Jedidja, Kamaya Painters, Kamui, Lagan Valley, Main Men, Major League, Manilla Rising, Paradise In Dubs, Pink Elephant, Steve Forte Rio, T-Scanner, TB X-Press, The Veil Kings, Two Deejays, Vimana, West & Storm

Private record label
Black Hole Recordings

Tijs Michiel Verwest cultivated his passion for music from the age of twelve. Having begun DJing professionally at school parties, before moving on to become a resident jockey at several clubs in the Netherlands between 1985 and 1994, it was at The Spock, a small club located in his hometown of Breda that he was able to fine-tune his own style by playing the backroom from ten PM until four AM on weekends. Back then, Verwest used to play mostly house, new beat and a good amount of Madonna songs.

In 1994, the young DJ and producer began releasing hardcore tracks under a variety of aliases such as Da Joker and DJ Limited, via the likes of Noculan Records sub-labels Chemo and Coolman.

Later that year, Verwest signed to Basic Beat, making friends with Arny Bink, founder of the Trashcan sub-division with whom he co-created another sub-branch, Guardian Angel, home to the acclaimed Forbidden Paradise series. The year 1995 marks the birth of his new persona and future legend, Tiësto: a nod to his childhood nickname with an Italian twist.

In the fall of 1997, Bink and Verwest chose to move on from Basic Beat to create their own record label, Black Hole Recordings. Verwest then met producer Dennis Waakop Reijers in 1998—who, alongside Geert Huinink, is credited as producer, writer, composer or arranger for various releases under the Tiësto alias.

A key release in his blooming career, Summerbreeze made for Tiësto's breakthrough mix compilation in the US thanks to a contract signed with Nettwerk. Appearing on the album, his remix of Silence by Delerium, featuring Sarah McLachlan on vocals, gave him significant exposure to a usually more mainstream audience.

Other notable productions from that early era include the DJ Tiësto singles Sparkles, Theme From Norefjell and The Tube, No More Tears as Allure,

Wasteland as Kamaya Painters (with Benno de Goeij) and Mirror as Stray Dog.

DJ Tiësto's steady rise to prominence was further reinforced by his now legendary DJ-set at the first edition of Innercity in Amsterdam in 1998. In the wake of this seminal event, two mix CD series were created—Magik and In Search Of Sunrise, resulting in seven compilations each, as well as Verwest's 2001-released debut full-length In My Memory, which included the singles Flight 643, Obsession (with Junkie XL) and Suburban Train.

International gigs started to pile up and his six-hour Tiësto Solo DJ-sets soon became in high demand. The release of a double mix CD titled Nyana further cemented Verwest's status as a leading trance curator on a global level. Nyana portrayed his DJ performances in both indoor and outdoor settings, meaning the pace went up and crossovers with more techno-oriented material were elaborated.

Not long after, Verwest was credited as the first DJ ever to have held a solo concert in a stadium. On May 10, 2003, Tiësto performed in front of twenty five thousand people at Arnhem's GelreDome. Verwest repeated that concert performance the following year on two consecutive nights and became the first DJ to play live on stage at the Olympic Games, when he performed at the opening ceremony of the Summer Olympics in Athens, Greece in 2004.

DJ Tiësto on Ibiza, 2000 © Pim Warnars

"I saw a DJ from Germany called Sven Väth. I saw him in the club, he played for six hours and I was just totally intrigued, because everything he played I'd never heard before and everything he did I'd never seen before. I was so blown away by what he did."

RELEASES

Music and its medium are undeniably linked. Although vinyl records have been around for decades before the first ever trance record came to life, the medium played a particularly important role in the development of the genre. New vinyl releases were not only sought after by DJs who were depending on them, but also became a much desired item for the enthusiast, being made available to an ever-growing audience than before.

Reissuing also played a major role in the visibility of the genre. Popular records were widely and continuously available—either via the parent label or via sub-licensing to other labels that would handle the production and distribution process within their respective regions. These reissues regularly featured an updated version of the original material, or included previously unreleased remixes. The widespread availability and large amount of pressings helped keep record prices low for decades to come, which makes the classic releases of the genre relatively easy to obtain on the second-hand market to this day.

Over the course of fifteen years, various records played a significant part in the growth of trance music. Moving from the inception of electronic music as a distinct scene in the early nineties into the peak mainstream popularity of trance around the mid-noughties, the following selection spans five hundred outstanding releases and is based on the perceived impact of these tracks in their respective era of production and/or release.

Each of these records either had a positive impact on the genre in musical terms (either at the time of releases, or in retrospect), found its way into the record bags of popular DJs, was on heavy rotation in clubs worldwide, managed to become a significant commercial success, or—in many cases—a combination of these elements. Emphasis is laid upon these releases that made a unique musical contribution to the genre on a wider scale.

These records were formed and shaped by devoted artists, whose joint efforts helped define the reach and level of success of the respective styles they fostered. Determined artists are necessary in exploring a genre's potential to the fullest, pushing the boundaries and forging meaningful collaborations that are set up with the purpose of generating artistic value.

Obviously, the said artists not only created the music at the root of a genre, but laid the foundations to sounds both unique and mutually reliant, outlining truly singular artistic visions both individually and collectively. In order to get a better understanding of the minds behind some of these influential releases, this chapter is dedicated to some of the most relevant artists to have navigated within the musical boundaries of trance music.

Although their backgrounds widely differ in nature, each of these artists created a benchmark for the sound of trance at some point in time. Their stories are not merely about success: rather, each story is aimed at framing their initial musical experiences and experiments, emphasising their devotion to following their inner passion and reaching their personal goals, while making a high-impact contribution to their musical community. These are stories about craftsmanship, creativity and involvement, but also about hard work, struggles, as well as liberation of relentless energy.

The label, catalogue, country and year tags generally refer to the first official vinyl pressing of the release, or to the version that gained popular appeal. Mix versions are only mentioned when different versions or (re)mixes are available for the stated release. Outlining a broad range of artists and titles, only one release per alias is featured in order to offer a larger overview of the genre's roots and shoots.

A

ABOVE & BEYOND
—Far From In Love
Label	Anjunabeats
Catalogue	ANJ009
Country	United Kingdom
Year	2001
A1	Far From In Love (Original Mix)
B1	Far From In Love (San Fransisco Mix)

ACCADIA
—Into The Dawn
Label	Lost Language
Catalogue	LOST006
Country	United Kingdom
Year	2001
A1	Into The Dawn (Ashtrax Mix)
B1	Into The Dawn (Accadia Club Mix)

ACCESSIVE RHYTHM
—Activate
Label	Maelstrom Records
Catalogue	MAELT022
Country	United Kingdom
Year	2001
A1	Activate
B1	Structural Beat

AFFIE YUSUF & NIGEL CASEY
—Mad Dogs And Englishmen
Label	909 Pervertions
Catalogue	PER910
Country	United Kingdom
Year	1994
A1	Leeds
A2	London
B1	Manchester
B2	Sheffield

AFTERBURN
—North Pole/Frattboy
Label	XtraBlue
Catalogue	X2B112
Country	United Kingdom
Year	2000
A1	North Pole
B1	Frattboy

AFROTRANCE
—Afrotrance
Label	R&S Records
Catalogue	RS93021
Country	Belgium
Year	1993
A1	Flying Dreams
A2	Deep Into The Dream
B1	Mental Vision
B2	Thousand Of Miles

AGE OF LOVE
—The Age Of Love
Label	React
Catalogue	12REACT9
Country	United Kingdom
Year	1992
A1	The Age Of Love (Watch Out For Stella Club Mix)
A2	The Age Of Love (Sign Of The Time Mix)
B1	The Age Of Love (OPM Mix)
B2	The Age Of Love (New Age Mix)
B3	The Age Of Love (Boeing Mix)

AGENT ORANGE
—More Love EP
Label	Loop Records
Catalogue	LOOP008
Country	Sweden
Year	1995
A1	More Acid
A2	Warm Love
B1	Give A Little More Love
B2	The Gong Of Love

AGNELLI & NELSON
—El Nino
Label	Xtravaganza Recordings
Catalogue	XTRAV0091570EXT
Country	United Kingdom
Year	1998
A1	El Nino (Matt Darey Remix)
B1	El Nino (Original Mix)

AIR LIQUIDE
—Liquide Air EP
Label	Blue
Catalogue	BLUE003
Country	Germany
Year	1992
A1	Liquid Air (Original Mix)
A2	Revelation
A3	Liquid Air (Bionaut Remix)
B1	Liquid Men With Liquid Hearts
B2	Psy 9
B3	Liquide Air (Xenon Remix)

AIRSCAPE
—L'Esperanza
Label	Xtravaganza Recordings
Catalogue	XTRAV712
Country	United Kingdom
Year	1999
A1	L'Esperanza (Original Mix)
B1	L'Esperanza (Sven Goes To The Love Parade—Extended Mix)

AIRWAVE
—Escape From Nowhere
Label	Bonzai Trance Progressive
Catalogue	BTP-66-2000
Country	Belgium
Year	2000
A1	Escape From Nowhere
B1	Alone In The Dark

ALBION
—Air
Label	Platipus
Catalogue	PLAT38
Country	United Kingdom
Year	1998

A1	Air (Original Mix)
B1	Air (Palefield Mountain Mix)

ALIBI
—Eternity

Label	Armind
Catalogue	ARM004
Country	Netherlands
Year	2000
A1	Eternity (Original IC Mix)
B1	Eternity (Armin van Buuren's Rising Star Mix)

ALLURE
—When She Left

Label	Planetary Consciousness
Catalogue	PC9804-6
Country	Germany
Year	1998
A1	When She Left (Wavestate Remix)
B1	When She Left (Original Mix)

ALPHAZONE
—Sunrise

Label	Waterworld
Catalogue	WWR021
Country	Germany
Year	2005
A1	Sunrise (Original Mix)
B1	Sunrise (Cygnific Remix)

AMBASSADOR
—The Fade

Label	Smash Trax
Catalogue	ST002
Country	Netherlands
Year	1999
A1	The Fade (Original Mix)
B1	The Fade (Fade Mix)

AMOEBA ASSASSIN
—Rollercoaster

Label	Perfecto
Catalogue	PERF163T
Country	United Kingdom
Year	1998
A1	Rollercoaster (Oakey's Courtyard Mix)
B1	Rollercoaster (Listen And Feel Live Mix)

ANDAIN
—Summer Calling

Label	Black Hole Recordings
Catalogue	BH140-5
Country	Netherlands
Year	2002
A1	Summer Calling (Josh Gabriel Mix)
B1	Summer Calling (Gabriel & Dresden Remix)

ANDROMEDA
—Trip To Space

Label	Save The Vinyl
Catalogue	S.T.V.010
Country	Germany
Year	1993
A1	Trip To Space
B1	Dream Frequencies

AQUAFORM
—El Sueno

Label	Eye Q Records
Catalogue	EYEQ018
Country	Germany
Year	1994
A1	El Sueno
B1	Borneo

AQUILIA
—Dreamstate

Label	Triple XXX Red
Catalogue	12TXR006R
Country	United Kingdom
Year	2000
A1	Dreamstate (L.S.G. Remix)
A2	Dreamstate (Aquilia's Alpha Mix)
B1	Dreamstate (Dakota Remix)

ARIA
—Dido/Willow

Label	Black Hole Recordings
Catalogue	BH117-5
Country	Netherlands
Year	2000
A1	Dido (Armin Van Buuren's Universal Religion Mix)
B1	Willow (DJ Tiësto's Magikal Remake)

ARMIN
—Blue Fear

Label	Cyber Records
Catalogue	CR015
Country	Netherlands
Year	1997
A1	Blue Fear
B1	X Marks The Spot
B2	Archeae From Space

ARPEGGIATORS
—Freedom Of Expression

Label	Harthouse
Catalogue	HH004
Country	Germany
Year	1992
A1	Freedom Of Expression
B1	Trancemission
B2	Helter Skelter

ART OF TRANCE
—Madagasga

Label	Platipus
Catalogue	PLAT43
Country	United Kingdom
Year	1998
A1	Madagasga (Original Mix)
B1	Madagasga (Cygnus X Remix)

ASCENSION
—Someone

Label	Perfecto
Catalogue	PERF141T
Country	United Kingdom

Year	1997
A1	Someone (Original Vocal Mix)
B1	Someone (Slacker's Rolling Mix)
B2	Someone (Slacker's Elevation Vocal)

ASIA 2001
—Guarana Cupana
Label	Trans'Pact Productions
Catalogue	VOL073
Country	France
Year	1994
A1	Guarana Cupana
B1	Arkology
B2	Guarana (Goa Beach Mix)

ASTRAL PROJECTION
—Dancing Galaxy/Ambient Galaxy (Disco Valley Mix)
Label	Transient Records
Catalogue	TRA037
Country	United Kingdom
Year	1997
A1	Dancing Galaxy
B1	Ambient Galaxy (Disco Valley Mix)

AT THE VILLA PEOPLE
—Open Your Eyes
Label	Made In DJ
Catalogue	MDJ65
Country	Spain
Year	1997
A1	Open Your Eyes (Extended Remix)
B1	Open Your Eyes (Short Version)

ATB
—9 PM (Till I Come)
Label	Kontor Records
Catalogue	KONTOR035
Country	Germany
Year	1998
A1	9 PM (9 PM Mix)
B1	9 PM (Original Mix)

ATLANTIC OCEAN
—Waterfall
Label	Eastern Bloc Records
Catalogue	BLOC001
Country	United Kingdom
Year	1993
A1	Waterfall (Original Mix)
A2	Waterfall (Deep Tranquil Mix)
B1	Waterfall (Ritmo Rivals Remix)
B2	Mimosa

ATLANTIS
—Fiji
Label	Spot On Records
Catalogue	SPOT32
Country	United Kingdom
Year	1999
A1	Fiji (Original Mix)
B1	Fiji (Cequenza Remix)

AURA
—Energy Transepose
Label	Impulse Recordings Inc.
Catalogue	IP0005
Country	Belgium
Year	1995
A1	Energy Transepose
B1	5th Dimension
B2	Mind Release

AURASFERE
—The Greenhouse Effect
Label	EXperimental
Catalogue	EX-25
Country	United States
Year	1994
A1	The Greenhouse Effect
B1	Terrasuave
C1	Sunrise On Epsilon
D1	For Simple Minds

AURORA BOREALIS
—The Milky Way
Label	F Communications
Catalogue	F003
Country	France
Year	1994
A1	The Milky Way
B1	The Milky Way (Lunatic Acid Mix)
B2	The Milky Way (Scan X Mix)

AYLA
—Ayla
Label	Maddog
Catalogue	INT128.099
Country	Germany
Year	1996
A1	Ayla (Original Mix)
A2	Ayla (Progressive-Version)
B1	Ayla (Club-Mix)
B2	Ambience

AYU
—M EP
Label	Avex Trax
Catalogue	AVJK-3040
Country	Japan
Year	2001
A1	M (Above & Beyond Typhoon Dub Mix)
B1	Boys & Girls (Push Instrumental Dub)
B2	Unite! (Airwave Dub)
C1	Unite! (Airwave Remix)
C2	Appears (Armin van Buuren's Sunset Dub)
D1	Unite! (Moogwai Dub)
D2	Audience (Darren Tate Instrumental)

AZZIDO DA BASS
—Dooms Night
Label	Club Tools
Catalogue	012028-0CLU
Country	Germany
Year	1999
A1	Dooms Night (Timo Maas Remix)
B1	Dooms Night (Pascal F.E.O.S. Treatment Mix)

B

BAD MAN
—Lover Man
Label	Prolekult
Catalogue	KULT007
Country	United Kingdom
Year	1995
A1	Lover Man (Original Mix)
B1	Lover Man (Another Mix)

BALIL
—Parasight
Label	Rising High Records
Catalogue	RSN72
Country	United Kingdom
Year	1993
A1	Rosery Pilots
A2	Avidya
B1	Parasight
B2	Island

BASIC GRAVITY
—Rajah
Label	Rising High Records
Catalogue	RSN94
Country	United Kingdom
Year	1994
A1	Rajah (Serious Mix)
B1	Rajah (Rise Mix)
B2	Rajah (Original Mix)

BALLROOM
—Passenger/Motherless Child
Label	Underworld Recordings
Catalogue	UW9619-12
Country	Germany
Year	2000
A1	Passenger (Marc O'Tool Remix)
B1	Motherless Child

BANCO DE GAIA
—Last Train To Lhasa
Label	Planet Dog
Catalogue	BARK010T
Country	United Kingdom
Year	1995
A1	Last Train To Lhasa (Original Mix)
B1	Last Train To Lhasa (Extended Ambient Mix)

BARBARELLA
—My Name Is Barbarella
Label	Eye Q Records
Catalogue	PRO725
Country	Germany
Year	1992
A1	My Name Is Barbarella
B1	Barbarella Butterfly
B2	The Mission

BEDROCK
—Heaven Scent
Label	Bedrock Records
Catalogue	BED1
Country	United Kingdom
Year	1999
A1	Heaven Scent (Original Mix)
B1	Heaven Scent (Evolution Dub Mix)

BERKANA SOWELU
—Solid Fuel
Label	Pacific Records
Catalogue	FIC001
Country	United Kingdom
Year	1994
A1	Solid Fuel
B1	Solid Fuel (Morph Remix)

BINARY FINARY
—1998
Label	Positiva
Catalogue	12TIV98
Country	United Kingdom
Year	1998
A1	1998 (Matt Darey Mix)
B1	1998 (Binary Finary Mix)
B2	1998 (Paul Van Dyk Remix)

BLANK & JONES
—Cream
Label	Deviant Records
Catalogue	DVNT31X
Country	Germany
Year	1999
A1	Cream (Long version)
B1	Cream (Paul van Dyk Mix)

BLUE ALPHABET
—Cybertrance
Label	Bonzai Records
Catalogue	BR94056
Country	Belgium
Year	1994
A1	Cybertrance
B1	Quixotism

BLUE MINDS
—The Beginning
Label	Aquablue Recordings
Catalogue	AQUA94001
Country	Belgium
Year	1994
A1	Aquapunch (3 In One Mix)
A2	Aquapunch (Global Mix)
B1	Eternal Heaven
B2	Vibrational Odysseys

BORA BORA
—Love Song
Label	S.O.B. (Sound Of The Bomb)
Catalogue	SOB195
Country	Italy
Year	1993
A1	Love Song (Guerrillas Mix)
B1	Love Song (Love Dub Mix)
B2	Love Song (Supreme Trance Mix)

BRAINBUG
—Rain
Label	Volumex
Catalogue	VOL198-11
Country	Italy
Year	1998

A1	Rain (Original Brainbug Mix)
A2	Rain (Johnny Vicious Mix)
B1	Rain (Perpetual Motion Mix)
B2	Rain (Cascade Mix)

BRAINCELL
—Hybrid EP
Label	Harthouse
Catalogue	HH031
Country	Germany
Year	1993
A1	Time Is Suspended
B1	Shapechanger
B2	Nimrod

BRAINCHILD
—Synfonica/Hypnotic Shuffle
Label	Eye Q Records
Catalogue	EYEQ009
Country	Germany
Year	1993
A1	Synfonica
B1	Hypnotic Shuffle

BREEDER
—Twilo Thunder
Label	Rhythm Syndicate Records
Catalogue	RHYSYN002
Country	United Kingdom
Year	1999
A1	Twilo Thunder (Stoked Up Mix)
B1	Beetlejuice (Version 4)

BT
—Flaming June
Label	Perfecto
Catalogue	PERF145T
Country	United Kingdom
Year	1997
A1	Flaming June (BT & PVD Mix)
B1	Flaming June (H.H.C. Remix)

B.B.E.
—Seven Days And One Week/Hypnose
Label	Triangle
Catalogue	TRI-V-96001
Country	Belgium
Year	1996
A1	Seven Days And One Week
B1	Hypnose

C

CANYON
—Planet Ten/Move
Label	Hook Recordings
Catalogue	HK008
Country	UK
Year	1996
A1	Planet Ten
B1	Move

CAPRICORN
—20 Hz
Label	Global Cuts
Catalogue	GC2
Country	Belgium
Year	1993
A1	20 Hz
B1	Didn't I
B2	For The Soul, Body & Mind

CARMINE SORRENTINO & DAVE CARLOTTI PRESENT: MISS JANE
—It's A Fine Day
Label	Hitland
Catalogue	HTL98.12
Country	Italy
Year	1998
A1	It's A Fine Day (ATB Club Remix)
A2	It's A Fine Day (ATB Radio Edit)
B1	It's A Fine Day (Original Clubby Mix)
B2	It's A Fine Day (C.J. Stone's Pleasure Remix)
B3	Angel's Song (Original Mix)

CASS & SLIDE
—Perception
Label	Automatic Records
Catalogue	AUTO15
Country	United Kingdom
Year	1999
A1	Perception
B1	3tyrants@thebonaparte

CAUCASUSS
—Caucasuss
Label	Le Petit Prince
Catalogue	PRINCE94/16
Country	Germany
Year	1994
A1	Me And My 303
A2	Our Dream
B1	Dream Scape
B2	Reversible Dreams

CAUNOS
—Herzsprung EP
Label	Le Petit Prince
Catalogue	PRINCE94/19
Country	Germany
Year	1994
A1	Herzsprung 1
B1	The Rhythm
B2	Chilliwack

CENITH X
—Feel
Label	3 Lanka
Catalogue	DMD3LAN-009
Country	Germany
Year	1995
A1	Feel (Legend B. Remix)
B1	Feel (SMP-Club Mix)
B2	Feel (CZ-101 Remix)

CEQUENZA
—Sonic Blue
Label	Spot On Records
Catalogue	SPOT45
Country	United Kingdom
Year	2001
A1	Sonic Blue (Cequenza Main Mix)

B1	Sonic Blue (John Johnson Remix)

CHAKRA
—Home
Label	Warner Elektra Atlantic
Catalogue	WEA116T
Country	United Kingdom
Year	1997
A1	Home (Original Mix)
A2	Home (Solar Stone Remix)
B1	Home (The Space Brothers Remix)
B2	Home (Salt Tank Reconstruction)

CHERRY BOMB
—Untitled
Label	Music Man Records
Catalogue	MM010
Country	Belgium
Year	1994
A1	Eclipse
A2	Trajectory
B1	Asylum
B2	Elastic

CHERRYMOON TRAX / SPACE MODULE
—Trax I
Label	Bonzai Records
Catalogue	BR94054
Country	Belgium
Year	1994
A1	Cherrymoon Trax —The House Of House
B1	Space Module—Dreamworld

CHICANE
—Offshore
Label	Modena Records
Catalogue	MOD003
Country	United Kingdom
Year	1996
A1	Offshore (Disco Citizens Remix)
B1	Offshore (Original Mix)

CHILLER TWIST
—Stringz Ultd.
Label	Plum Projects
Catalogue	SPLUMT005
Country	United Kingdom
Year	2001
A1	Stringz Ultd. (Shelley Mix)
B1	Stringz Ultd. (Baptism Mix)

CHOICE/SOOFLE
—Acid Eiffel/How Do You Plead?
Label	Fragile Records
Catalogue	FRG-6
Country	United States
Year	1993
A1	Choice—Acid Eiffel
B1	Soofle—How Do You Plead?

CHRIS LAKE
—Santiago De Cuba
Label	Lost Language
Catalogue	LOST017
Country	United Kingdom
Year	2002
A1	Santiago De Cuba (Original Mix)
B1	Santiago De Cuba (Jürgen Driessen Remix)

CIRCUIT
—Transport Of Love
Label	Frankfurt Beat Productions
Catalogue	901029.6
Country	Germany
Year	1994
A1	Transport Of Love
B1	Mental Atmosphere
B2	Parametic Values

CLANGER
—Clanger/Seadog
Label	Seismic Records
Catalogue	SMC005
Country	United Kingdom
Year	1994
A1	Clanger
B1	Seadog

CLASSIFIED PROJECT
—Resurrection
Label	District Records
Catalogue	DISTRICT001
Country	Netherlands
Year	1998
A1	Resurrection (Amsterdam Club Mix)
A2	Resurrection (Original Mix)
B1	Subculture (Relaxation Mix)

CLOUD 69
—Sixty Nine Ways
Label	XTC
Catalogue	XTC053
Country	Belgium
Year	2000
A1	Sixty Nine Ways
B1	When I Close My Eyes

COAST 2 COAST FEATURING DISCOVERY
—Home
Label	Free For All
Catalogue	7004055
Country	Netherlands
Year	2001
A1	Home (Original Mix)
B1	Home (5 AM Remix)

COLOGNE SUMMER
—Cologne Summer EP
Label	Le Petit Prince
Catalogue	PRINCE93/04
Country	Germany
Year	1993
A1	Brasilian Mouthwash
A2	The Man From Gaza
B1	Brasilian Mouthwash (Alici Remix)
B2	Sunshower

COLOURED VISION
—Violet Rain
Label	Plasma Records

Catalogue	RTD364.1001.0
Country	Germany
Year	1993
A1	Violet Rain (139.2014 BPM Mix)
B1	Living In Paradise (The Eagle Has Landed Mix)

COMMANDER TOM
—Volume One
Label	Noom Records
Catalogue	NOOM013-6
Country	Germany
Year	1995
A1	Are Am Eye?
B1	Round My Brain
B2	Eternity (To Yazzy)

CONFESSION
—I Found My Love
Label	Abfahrt Records
Catalogue	ABF0007-12
Country	Germany
Year	1992
A1	I Found My Love (Trance Mix)
B1	I Found My Love (Club Mix)

CONJURE ONE FEATURING SINÉAD O'CONNOR
—Tears From The Moon
Label	Nettwerk America
Catalogue	067003317313
Country	United States
Year	2002
A1	Tears From The Moon (Tiësto In Search Of Sunrise Remix)
B1	Tears From The Moon (Hybrid Twisted On The Terrace Dub)

COSMIC BABY
—Fantasia
Label	Logic Records
Catalogue	LOC144
Country	Germany
Year	1994
A1	Fantasia (Celestial Harmonies)
B1	Fantasia (Talking Drums)
B2	Fantasia (Remix II)

COSMIC GATE
—Exploration Of Space/Melt To The Ocean
Label	EMI Electrola
Catalogue	724388975162
Country	Germany
Year	2000
A1	Exploration Of Space
B1	Melt To The Ocean

CRESCENDO
—Are You Out There
Label	Full Frequency Range Recordings
Catalogue	FX270
Country	United Kingdom
Year	1995
A1	Are You Out There (Original Mix)
B1	Are You Out There (Movements 1 To 5) (Alternative Mix)

CRW
—I Feel Love
Label	Inside Label
Catalogue	IN6126
Country	Italy
Year	1998
A1	I Feel Love (Extended Mix)
B1	I Feel Love (Clubby Mix)

CYBERIA
—Mr. Chill's Back
Label	IST Records
Catalogue	IST001
Country	United States
Year	1993
A1	Mr. Chill's Back (Door 1)
A2	Mr. Chill's Back (Door 2)
B1	Mr. Chill's Back (Door 3)

CYBERNAUT
—Hydrophonix/Califrae
Label	Intastella Records
Catalogue	INTA07
Country	United Kingdom
Year	1997
A1	Hydrophonix
B1	Califrae (Colourful Mix)
B2	Califrae (Original Mix)

CYBORDELICS
—Nighthorse
Label	Harthouse
Catalogue	HH026
Country	Germany
Year	1993
A1	Adventures Of Dama
B1	First Trip

CYGNUS X
—The Orange Theme
Label	Eye Q Records
Catalogue	EYEQ022
Country	Germany
Year	1994
A1	The Orange Theme
B1	Introspective

CYTAX
—Deep Dream EP
Label	Pedo Beat Records
Catalogue	PB940003-1
Country	Germany
Year	1994
A1	Deep Dream
A2	Acid Escape
B1	Traumatic
B2	Fastcinate

D

DA HOOL
—Meet Her At The Love Parade
Label	Kosmo Records
Catalogue	KOS008
Country	Germany
Year	1997
A1	Meet Her At The Love Parade (Nalin & Kane Remix)

B1	Meet Her At The Love Parade (Espanol Vocal Dub)
B2	Meet Her At The Love Parade (Original Mix)

DANCE 2 TRANCE
—We Came In Peace
Label	Logic Records
Catalogue	7432117375-1
Country	United Kingdom
Year	1993
A1	We Came In Peace ('93 Mix)
B1	We Came In Peace (Original '90 Mix)
B2	We Came In Peace ('91 Mix)

DARUDE
—Sandstorm
Label	Neo
Catalogue	NEO12033
Country	United Kingdom
Year	1999
A1	Sandstorm (Original Mix)
B1	Sandstorm (JS16 Remix)

DATURA
—Eternity
Label	Trance Records
Catalogue	LSD015
Country	Italy
Year	1993
A1	Eternity (Samsara)
A2	Eternity (Nirvana)
B1	Eternity (Nidana)
B2	West Line

DAVID FORBES
—Questions Must Be Asked
Label	Eve Records
Catalogue	EVE00035
Country	United Kingdom
Year	2000
A1	Questions Must Be Asked
B1	Safe

DAWNSEEKERS
—Gothic Dream
Label	Platipus
Catalogue	PLAT77
Country	United Kingdom
Year	2000
A1	Gothic Dream (Original Mix)
B1	Gothic Dream (John Johnson Remix)

DEE REX
—Soilent Green/Soilent Blue
Label	Lunatec
Catalogue	LUNA017
Country	Germany
Year	1995
A1	Soilent Green
B1	Soilent Blue

DEEPSKY
—Stargazer EP
Label	Fragrant Music
Catalogue	FRA015
Country	US
Year	1999
A1	Stargazer (Deepsky's Retroactive Mix)
B1	Stargazer (X-Cabs Mix)

DELERIUM
—Silence
Label	Nettwerk
Catalogue	5037703310612
Country	United Kingdom
Year	1999
A1	Silence (Airscape Remix)
B1	Silence (DJ Tiësto's In Search Of Sunrise Remix)

DER DRITTE RAUM
—Hale Bopp
Label	Virgin
Catalogue	724389525663
Country	Germany
Year	1998
A1	Hale Bopp
B1	Infrarot

DESERT STORM
—Desert Storm/Scoraig 93
Label	Soma Quality Recordings
Catalogue	SOMA013
Country	United Kingdom
Year	1994
A1	Desert Storm
B1	Scoraig 93

DIFFUSION
—Even Moaning/Lushes
Label	EXperimental
Catalogue	EX-22
Country	United States
Year	1993
A1	Even Moaning
B1	Lushes

DIGITAL JUSTICE
—Theme From: Its All Gone Pearshaped
Label	Fragile Records
Catalogue	FRG-14
Country	United States
Year	1996
A1	Theme From: Its All Gone Pearshaped
B1	Alternative Reality: Part 1: Shapes

DIMENSION
—Dimension EP
Label	Azwan Transmissions
Catalogue	AZWAN-012
Country	Australia
Year	1994
A1	Progress
A2	White Dove
B1	Ascention To Altitude

DIMENSION 5
—Deep Space 5D/Temple Of Chaos

Label	Intastella Records	B2	U (W-Mix)
Catalogue	INTA06	B3	U (X-Mix)
Country	United Kingdom		
Year	1997		
A1	Deep Space 5D		
B1	Temple Of Chaos		

DJ TIËSTO
—Theme From Norefjell

Label	Black Hole Recordings
Catalogue	BH106-5
Country	Netherlands
Year	1999
A1	Theme From Norefjell (Magikal Remake)
B1	Theme From Norefjell (DJ Jan & Christophe Chantzis Mix)

DJ ALBERT VS. PRECISION
—Say Yes

Label	Silver Premium
Catalogue	SP-080
Country	Netherlands
Year	2002
A1	Say Yes (Silent Mix)
B1	Say Yes (Dub Mix)

DJ COR FIJNEMAN FEATURING JAN JOHNSTON
—Venus (Meant To Be Your Lover)

Label	In Trance We Trust
Catalogue	ITWT352-5
Country	Netherlands
Year	2003
A1	Venus (Meant To Be Your Lover) (Tiësto Remix)
B1	Venus (Meant To Be Your Lover) (DJ Cor Fijneman's Outstanding Mix)

DJ DADO
—X-Files

Label	Subway Records
Catalogue	SUB116
Country	Italy
Year	1996
A1	X-Files (DJ Dado Paranormal Activity Mix)
A2	X-Files (Claudio Diva Sub-Dream Activity Mix)

DJ POSEIDON
—Supertransonic

Label	Hope Recordings
Catalogue	HOPE013
Country	United Kingdom
Year	2000
A1	Supertransonic (Jody Wayoutwest Mix)
B1	Supertransonic (Timo Maas Mix)

DJ REMY
—Home Again/Backstabber

Label	Taste Recordings
Catalogue	TASTE020
Country	Netherlands
Year	1999
A1	Home Again
B1	Backstabber

DJ SCOT PROJECT
—U

Label	Overdose
Catalogue	DOSE018
Country	Germany
Year	1995
A1	U (V-Mix)
B1	U (U-Mix)

DNTEL
—(This Is) The Dream Of Evan And Chan

Label	Plug Research
Catalogue	PR360204
Country	United States
Year	2002
A1	(This Is) The Dream Of Evan And Chan (Original Version)
A2	(This Is) The Dream Of Evan And Chan (Safety Scissors Spilled My Drink Mix)
A3	(This Is) The Dream Of Evan And Chan (Barbara Morgenstern Remix)
B1	(This Is) The Dream Of Evan And Chan (Superpitcher Kompakt Remix)
B2	(This Is) The Dream Of Evan And Chan (Lali Puna Remix)

DOMINIC PLAZA
—Sounds Rushing

Label	Fokused Recordings
Catalogue	FKSD001
Country	Sweden
Year	2005
A1	Sounds Rushing (David West Remix)
B1	Sounds Rushing (Original Mix)

DOOF
—Disposable Hymns To The Infinite

Label	NovaMute
Catalogue	12NOMU11
Country	United Kingdom
Year	1993
A1	Gift Of The Gods
A2	In Flight
B1	The Nagual

DOVE BEAT
—La Paloma

Label	Sounds Good Records
Catalogue	SGR010
Country	Germany
Year	1997
A1	La Paloma (Ocean Mix)
B1	Coffee Drive (Comlete Mix)
B2	La Paloma (Dove Dub)

DRAX
—Drax Ltd. II

Label	Trope Recordings

Catalogue	TROPE008
Country	Germany
Year	1994
A1	Amphetamine
A2	The Silent Meadow
A3	Acid Generation
B1	Mindspawn
B2	Outdoor Excursions
B3	The Fight Goes On

DREAM CRASHER
−Forest Dream

Label	Subway Records
Catalogue	SUB105
Country	Italy
Year	1995
A1	Forest Dream (Heart Mix)
A2	Forest Dream (Mental Mix)
B1	Minimal Rain (Out Of Mind 1)
B2	Minimal Rain (Out Of Mind 2)

DREAM TRAVELER
−Time

Label	Dream Music
Catalogue	DM001
Country	United States
Year	1998
A1	Time (Original Mix)
B1	Time (Inertia's Dream Mix)

DREAMATIC
−I Can Feel It/Audio Trip

Label	DFC
Catalogue	DFC050
Country	Italy
Year	1991
A1	I Can Feel It (Pt. 1)
A2	I Can Feel It (Pt. 2)
B1	Audio Trip

DREAMCATCHER
−I Don't Wanna Lose My Way

Label	Kosmo Records
Catalogue	KOS2025
Country	Germany
Year	2001
A1	I Don't Wanna Lose My Way (Moguai Mix)
A2	I Don't Wanna Lose My Way (Divide & Rule Mix)
B1	I Don't Wanna Lose My Way (Praha Remix)

DR. ATOMIC
−Schudelfloss

Label	Guerilla
Catalogue	GRRR42
Country	United Kingdom
Year	1993
A1	Schudelfloss (High On Hedonism Mix)
B1	Schudelfloss (Dentalfloss Dub Mix)
B2	Schudelfloss (Original Full-On Goof Bump Mix)

DR. FERNANDO!
−Closer

Label	Music Man Records
Catalogue	MMI9387
Country	Belgium
Year	1993
A1	Closer
A2	4-3H(N)
B1	High Pressure
B2	Escape

DUTCH FORCE
−Deadline

Label	Insolent Tracks
Catalogue	INSMX131
Country	Spain
Year	1999
A1	Deadline (Extended Version)
B1	Deadline (Full Vocal Radio Mix)
B2	Till Midnight (Extended)

D.I.D.
−Alcyone

Label	Buzz
Catalogue	BZZXL106093
Country	Belgium
Year	1992
A1	Alcyone/Orbital Walk (Multi Rhythmic V.1.)
B1	Hyperion/Protesting Nature (Beat Version)
B2	Alcyone/Orbital Walk (Spatial V.2.)

D'NOTE
−Shed My Skin

Label	Ultralab
Catalogue	5460446
Country	Italy
Year	2001
A1	Shed My Skin (Pete Heller's Stylus Dub)
A2	Shed My Skin (Pete Heller's Stylus Mix)
B1	Shed My Skin (Original Mix)
B2	Shed My Skin (PMT Remix)
B3	Shed My Skin (Radio Edit)

D-GENERATION
−Una Musica Senza Ritmo

Label	Blue Cue Records
Catalogue	BC129201-1
Country	Germany
Year	1992
A1	Una Musica Senza Ritmo (Radio Edit)
A2	Una Musica Senza Ritmo (Menta Club Mix)
B1	Una Musica Senza Ritmo (Nina In Trance Mix)
B2	Feel The Melody (Moog Mix)

EBI
−Hi EP
Label	Space Teddy
Catalogue	ST006
Country	Germany
Year	1994
A1	Hi
A2	San
B1	You
B2	Shou

EARTH NATION
−An Artificial Dream
Label	Eye Q Records
Catalogue	0630-12486-0
Country	Germany
Year	1995
A1	An Artificial Dream (Glacier Mix)
A2	An Artificial Dream (Hallucinogen's Dragonfly Remix)
B1	An Artificial Dream (Sonic Phase Mix)

EAT STATIC
−Inanna
Label	Alien Records
Catalogue	AR-1
Country	United Kingdom
Year	1991
A1	Inanna
B1	Medicine Wheel

EDEN TRANSMISSION
−I'm So High
Label	Exist Dance
Catalogue	ED005
Country	United States
Year	1991
A1	I'm So High (Original Mix)
A2	I'm So High (Ubud Mix)
B1	Transmission: Maya
B2	Powertrance

ELECTRIC UNIVERSE
−Solar Energy EP
Label	Spirit Zone Recordings
Catalogue	SPIRITZONE4002
Country	Germany
Year	1994
A1	Solar Energy
A2	Electromagnetism
B1	Neutron Dance
B2	Cosmic Synphony

ELECTROVOYA
−Effervesce/Emotional Response
Label	Fundamental Recordings
Catalogue	FUN517
Country	Netherlands
Year	2004
A1	Effervesce
B1	Emotional Response

ELEVATOR
−Elevator
Label	Fax +49-69/450464
Catalogue	PS08/35
Country	Germany
Year	1994
A1	Isolazione
B1	Distruttibile−303
B2	La Mania

ENERGY 52
−Café Del Mar
Label	Eye Q Records
Catalogue	EYEQ001
Country	Germany
Year	1993
A1	Café Del Mar (DJ Kid Paul Mix)
B1	Café Del Mar (Cosmic Baby's Impression)

ENVIO
−Touched By The Sun
Label	A State Of Trance
Catalogue	ASOT007
Country	Netherlands
Year	2003
A1	Touched By The Sun (Original Mix)
B1	Touched By The Sun (Envio's Sunrise Remix)
B2	Touched By The Sun (Rusch & Elusive's Chill-Out Mix)

EON
−Pocket Damage
Label	Tsunami
Catalogue	TSU6034
Country	Netherlands
Year	2002
A1	Pocket Damage
B1	Talk To Me

EPHEDRA
−Eve
Label	Frankfurt Beat Productions
Catalogue	901001.6
Country	Germany
Year	1993
A1	Eve (Ceres Mix)
B1	Eve (Isis Mix)
B2	Vamos!

ESCAPE
−Escape
Label	Fax +49-69/450464
Catalogue	PK08/23
Country	Germany
Year	1992
A1	Escape To Earth
B1	Escape From Earth

ESSENTIAL CHROME
−Us & Them
Label	Logic Records
Catalogue	79591-59027-1
Country	United States
Year	1995
A1	Us & Them
B1	Mika

B2	The Making

ESTELLE
—Estelle EP
Label	Raum Records
Catalogue	None
Country	Germany
Year	1994
A1	Analogue Ice
A2	Harmonika
B1	Synch-Session

ESTUERA
—Tales From The South
Label	Magik Muzik
Catalogue	MM819-5
Country	Netherlands
Year	2004
A1	Tales From The South
B1	City Lights

ETA BETA J.
—On The Road
Label	S.O.B. (Sound Of The Bomb)
Catalogue	SOB252
Country	Italy
Year	1996
A1	On The Road (Original Mix)
A2	On The Road (Trance Mix)
B1	Eternal Dream
B2	The Second Dimension

ETNICA
—Tribute/Astral Way
Label	Blue Room Released
Catalogue	BR010
Country	United Kingdom
Year	1995
A1	Tribute
B1	Astral Way

ETNICA GROUP
—The EP
Label	Brainstorm
Catalogue	BRA024
Year	1994
A1	Gollum
A2	Fingers
B1	Big Dust In Chapora Fort

EVE
—Riser
Label	Pacifica Recordings
Catalogue	PR4
Country	Untied Kingdom
Year	1999
A1	Riser (Original Mix)
B1	Riser (Christian West Mix)

EVOLUTION
—Untitled
Label	Gaia Tonträger
Catalogue	GT005
Country	Germany
Year	1993
A1	The Experience Of Taking A Step Into Someones Dream
B1	Sub-Marine
B2	Tribalism

EXIT EEE
—Epidemic
Label	No Respect Records
Catalogue	NRR018
Country	Germany
Year	1993
A1	Epidemic (Straight From Heaven Mix)
B1	Wheels Of Motion

EXTREME TRAX
—Final Fantasy
Label	XTC
Catalogue	XTC026
Country	Belgium
Year	1998
A1	Final Fantasy
B1	I'm Gonna Get You
B2	Big Sleep

EYAL BARKAN & A-FORCE
—Revolution
Label	In Trance We Trust
Catalogue	ITWT337-5
Country	Netherlands
Year	2002
A1	Revolution (Eyal Barkan Extended)
B1	Revolution (DJ Cor Fijneman Remix)

E.N.E.R.G.Y.
—Desire
Label	XTC
Catalogue	XTC056
Country	Belgium
Year	2000
A1	Desire (Original E.N.E.R.G.Y. Mix)
B1	Desire (Power Mix)

E-RAZOR
—Mantra/Yeti
Label	Technogold
Catalogue	TEG007-6
Country	Germany
Year	1997
A1	Mantra
B1	Yeti

E-RECTION
—Suck My Dang-A-Long
Label	Trigger
Catalogue	TR001
Country	Germany
Year	1992
A1	Suck My Dang-A-Long
B1	Smoke My Dang-A-Long

F

FADE
—... For All The People/All I Got

Label	Fade Records
Catalogue	FD001
Country	United States
Year	1994
A1	... For All The People
B1	All I Got

FAITHLESS
—Insomnia
Label	Cheeky Records
Catalogue	CHEK12.010
Country	United Kingdom
Year	1995
A1	Insomnia (Monster Mix)
B1	Insomnia (Moody Mix)

FATHERS OF SOUND FEATURING SHARON MAY LYNN
—Water
Label	Renaissance
Catalogue	REN001
Country	United Kingdom
Year	1998
A1	Water (Fathers Of Sound Main Vocal Mix)
B1	Water (The Light 12" Remix)
B2	Water (Parks & Wilson H2O Remix)

FERRY CORSTEN
—Punk
Label	Tsunami
Catalogue	TSU6031
Country	Netherlands
Year	2002
A1	Punk (Vocal Extended)
B1	Punk (Kid Vicious Remix)

FICTIVISION VS. C-QUENCE
—Symbols
Label	In Trance We Trust
Catalogue	ITWT354-5
Country	Netherlands
Year	2003
A1	Symbols (Original Mix)
B1	Symbols (Mesh Remix)

FILTERHEADZ
—Yimanya
Label	ID&T
Catalogue	7008015
Country	Netherlands
Year	2004
A1	Yimanya (Original Mix)
B1	Yimanya (TDR Remix)

FIRE & ICE
—Lost Emotions
Label	XTC
Catalogue	XTC027
Country	Belgium
Year	1998
A1	Lost Emotions
A2	Outer Space
B1	Antarctica (Land Of Illusions)
B2	Antarctica (Original Mix)

FORMIC ACID
—Dreams Of Fantasy
Label	ZYX Music
Catalogue	ZYX8023-12
Country	Germany
Year	1996
A1	Acid Dreams
A2	Trance Dreams
B1	Endless Dreams
B2	Ambient Dreams

FREAKY CHAKRA
—Year 2000
Label	Astralwerks
Catalogue	ASW6188
Country	United States
Year	1997
A1	Year 2000
A2	Dreams
B1	Platform
B2	Year 2000 (Love From San Francisco Mix)

FRED BAKER AND VINCENT GORCZAK
—La Part Des Anges
Label	A State Of Trance
Catalogue	ASOT044
Country	Netherlands
Year	2005
A1	La Part Des Anges (Original Mix)
B1	La Part Des Anges (Siberian Sun Remix)
B2	Little Star

FREEFALL FEATURING JAN JOHNSTON
—Skydive
Label	Stress Records
Catalogue	12STR89
Country	United Kingdom
Year	1998
A1	Skydive (Original Mix)
B1	Skydive (Whatadubaswell?)

FREE RADICAL
—Surreal
Label	A Trance Communication Release
Catalogue	TCOM007
Country	United Kingdom
Year	2000
A1	Surreal (En Motion Mix)
B1	Surreal (Free Radical Mix)

FRIDGE
—Paradise
Label	Go For It
Catalogue	GOFO9837-6
Country	Germany
Year	1998
A1	Paradise (Gray Mix)
B1	Paradise (Slipstream Mix)
B2	Paradise (Gate To Heaven)

FRIENDS, LOVERS & FAMILY
—Tribute EP
Label	Lush Recordings
Catalogue	LUSH02
Year	1995

A1	Tribute (Bucket & Spades)
B1	F.I.T.C.
B2	Assembly

FUTURE BREEZE
—Temple Of Dreams

Label	Alpha+
Catalogue	ABCD0101-6
Country	Germany
Year	2001
A1	Temple Of Dreams (Club Mix)
B1	Temple Of Dreams (Dub Mix)

FUTURESHOCK
—Frequency (The Return ...)

Label	Fuju
Catalogue	FUJU009
Country	United Kingdom
Year	2002
A1	Frequency (Original Mix)
B1	Frequency (Phil Kieran Mix)

G

GAIA
—4 Elements

Label	Captivating Sounds
Catalogue	CVS004
Country	Netherlands
Year	2000
A1	4 Elements (Extended Version)
B1	4 Elements (Chris Raven Remix)

GENLOG
—Airwalk

Label	Low Spirit Recordings
Catalogue	851951-1
Country	Germany
Year	1995
A1	Airwalk
B1	Airwalk (Total Control)

GIGI D'AGOSTINO/DANIELE MAFFEI
—Noise Maker Theme/Catodic Tube

Label	NoiseMaker
Catalogue	NM001
Country	Italy
Year	1994
A1	Gigi D'Agostino —Noise Maker Theme
B1	Daniele Maffei —Catodic Tube (Gas Gas Version)

GOAHEAD
—Free Beach

Label	Eye Q Records
Catalogue	EYEQ012
Country	Germany
Year	1993
A1	Freebeach (Anjuna Mix)
B1	Freebeach (Candolyn Mix)

GODAZIA
—The First Wave

Label	Faktory
Catalogue	FAK6004
Country	Belgium
Year	1999
A1	The First Wave (Original)
B1	The First Wave (DJ Glenn Mix)

GOLDENSCAN
—Sunrise

Label	VC Recordings
Catalogue	VCRT79
Country	United Kingdom
Year	2000
A1	Sunrise (Original Mix)
B1	Sunrise (DJ Tiësto Remix)

GOURYELLA
—Gouryella

Label	Tsunami
Catalogue	TSU6009
Country	Netherlands
Year	1999
A1	Gouryella
B1	Gorella

GREEN ATLAS
—Circulation

Label	Tatsumaki
Catalogue	TATS1703
Country	Netherlands
Year	2004
A1	Circulation
B1	Communicate

GREEN COURT FEATURING DE/VISION
—Shining/Trancefiguration

Label	Logport Recordings
Catalogue	DMDLOG2001
Country	Germany
Year	2000
A1	Shining (Sunshine Club Mix)
B1	Trancefiguration
B2	Shining (Marc Dawn Mix)

GTR
—Mistral

Label	Five AM
Catalogue	FAM17
Country	United Kingdom
Year	2002
A1	Mistral (Original Mix)
B1	Mistral (Ca-Lo's Creation Mix)

GUS GUS
—Purple

Label	4AD
Catalogue	GUS12
Country	United Kingdom
Year	1998
A1	Purple (Sasha V The Light)
B1	Polyesterday (Single Edit)

H

HALLUCINOGEN
—Alpha Centauri/LSD

Label	Dragonfly Records
Catalogue	BFLT14
Country	United Kingdom
Year	1994

A1	Alpha Centauri
B1	LSD

HAMMER & BENNETT
—Language
Label	Supra Recordings
Catalogue	SUPRA010
Country	Germany
Year	2005
A1	Language (Santiago Nino Dub Tech Mix)
B1	Language (Elevation Remix) (Markus Schulz Edit)
B2	Language (Original Mix)

HAMMOCK BROTHERS
—Blaze Of Night
Label	Trance Energy Records
Catalogue	TRANCE003
Country	Netherlands
Year	1998
A1	Blaze Of Night
B1	Earth
B2	Dwell Out In

HARMON EYES
—Through The Tunnel
Label	Loop Records
Catalogue	LOOP016
Country	Sweden
Year	1995
A1	Through The Tunnel
B1	Hop O' My Thumb
B2	Sensaesa

HH
—Spectrum EP
Label	Planetary Consciousness
Catalogue	PC9803-6
Country	Germany
Year	1998
A1	Take Me Higher (Original)
A2	Take Me Higher (Remixed by the "Laurence T. Sofer Crew")
B1	Planetary
B2	Train-Inc.

HOLDEN & THOMPSON
—Nothing
Label	Loaded Records
Catalogue	LOAD98
Country	United Kingdom
Year	2003
A1	Nothing (Original Mix)
B1	Nothing (93 Returning Mix)

HOLE IN ONE
—Life's Too Short EP
Label	Nutrition
Catalogue	NUT019
Country	Netherlands
Year	1996
A1	Life's Too Short (Too Short Mix)
B1	Full Ranks (In Your Mind) (Original Mix)
B2	Life's Too Short (Live At Paleis Soestdijk Mix)

HUMAN EVOLUTION
—Human Evolution
Label	ID&T
Catalogue	7005025
Country	Netherlands
Year	2002
A1	Human Evolution (Club Mix)
B1	Human Evolution (Vocal Mix)

HUMATE
—Love Stimulation/Curious
Label	MFS
Catalogue	MFS7034-0
Country	Germany
Year	1993
A1	Love Stimulation (Lovemix)
A2	Love Stimulation (Original Mix)
B1	Curious (Inquisitive Remix)
B2	Curious (Original Mix)

HYBRID
—Finished Symphony
Label	Distinct'ive Records
Catalogue	DISNST52
Country	United Kingdom
Year	1999
A1	Finished Symphony (Original Mix)
B1	Finished Symphony (Echoplex Remix)

HYPNOPEDIA
—Spectral EP
Label	BOY Records
Catalogue	BOY8846-12
Country	Germany
Year	1992
A1	Cario
A2	Mark IV
B1	Eclypse
B2	Spectral

HYPNOSIS
—Acid Before
Label	Made In Frankfurt
Catalogue	DMDFFM08
Country	Germany
Year	1996
A1	Random Believe
B1	Acid Before (Factor Mix)
B2	Acid Before (48 Inc. Mix)

IBERIAN
—Manufactured EP
Label	F Communications
Catalogue	F029
Country	France
Year	1995
A1	Crusher
A2	Is Up To U
A3	Darius
B1	Night Bird
B2	After Us

ICON
—Desire

Label	Eye Q Records
Catalogue	EYEQ014
Country	Germany
Year	1994
A1	Desire (Icarus Mix)
B1	Desire (Tronic Mix)

IIO
−Rapture
Label	Rise
Catalogue	RISE161
Country	Italy
Year	2001
A1	Rapture (Original Version)
A2	Rapture (John Creamer & Stephane K. Remix)
B1	Rapture (Radio Edit)
B2	Rapture (Deep Dish Miami Dub)

ILLEGAL DISTRICT
−My Dream
Label	Save The Vinyl
Catalogue	S.T.V.017
Country	Germany
Year	1994
A1	My Dream (Dream Mix)
B1	My Dream (Let Us Mix)
B2	My Dream (101303 Mix)

ILLUMINATAE
−Tremora Del Terra
Label	XVX
Catalogue	XVX·I
Country	United Kingdom
Year	1993
A1	Tremora Del Terra
B1	Dreammer (Club)
B2	Dreammer (Acid)

ILLUMINATUS
−Hope & Despair
Label	23 Frankfurt
Catalogue	23-004
Country	Germany
Year	1993
A1	Hope (Trance Mix)
A2	... Hope... Revisited
B1	Hope & Despair

INFECTED MUSHROOM
−Classical Mushroom EP
Label	Balloonia Ltd.
Catalogue	BALLLP-012
Country	Germany
Year	2000
A1	Sailing In The Sea Of Mushroom
B1	Mush Mushi
B2	None Of This Is Real

INFLEXION
−Pure
Label	Neo
Catalogue	NEO12015
Country	United Kingdom
Year	1999
A1	Pure (The Original Balearic Mix)
B1	Pure (The Olmec Heads Remix)

INFLUX
−Braineater
Label	Sapho
Catalogue	SAPH14
Country	United Kingdom
Year	1993
A1	Braineater
A2	Dreamscape
B1	Tiny Green Spots
B2	Vs 128

INSIGMA
−Open Our Eyes
Label	A Trance Communication Release
Catalogue	TCOM009
Country	United Kingdom
Year	2000
A1	Open Our Eyes (Insigma Mix)
B1	Open Our Eyes (Odyssey One Mix)

INTERSTATE
−I Found You
Label	Bandung
Catalogue	BNDG003
Country	Netherlands
Year	2005
A1	I Found You (Original Mix)
B1	I Found You (Harry Lemon Remix)

J

JAM & SPOON
−Tales From A Danceographic Ocean
Label	R&S Records
Catalogue	RS9203
Country	Belgium
Year	1992
A1	Stella
A2	Keep On Movin'
B1	My First Fantastic F.F.

JAN JOHNSTON
−Flesh
Label	Perfecto
Catalogue	PERF05TX
Country	United Kingdom
Year	2001
A1	Flesh (DJ Tiësto Remix)
B1	Flesh (Tilt's Going Home Mix)

JAVA
−1
Label	Eye Q Records
Catalogue	EYEQ011
Country	Germany
Year	1993
A1	Cosmos (C-Mix)
B1	Cosmos (Original Mix)
B2	Cosmos Chill

JERICHO
−Personal Reflexion
Label	Progrez
Catalogue	PRG005
Country	Belgium
Year	2002
A1	Personal Reflexion (Trance Mix)

B1	Personal Reflexion (Original Mix)

JOHAN GIELEN PRESENTS ABNEA
—Velvet Moods
Label	Data Records
Catalogue	DATA17T
Country	United Kingdom
Year	2001
A1	Velvet Moods (Native Remix)
B1	Velvet Moods (Tiësto's In Search Of Sunrise Remix)
B2	Velvet Moods (Original Mix)

JOHN '00' FLEMING
—Lost In Emotion
Label	React
Catalogue	12REACT170
Country	United Kingdom
Year	1999
A1	Lost In Emotion (Club Mix)
B1	Lost In Emotion (Angelic Vocal Mix)

JOKER JAM
—Innocence
Label	Red Series
Catalogue	RS1
Country	Germany
Year	2001
A1	Innocence (Planisphere Remix)
B1	Innocence (Tribal Mix)
B2	Innocence (Chill-Out Intro)

JON VESTA
—Gull/Bluestone
Label	Stonehouse Records
Catalogue	STONE001
Country	United Kingdom
Year	1999
A1	Gull
B1	Bluestone

JONES & STEPHENSON
—The First Rebirth
Label	Bonzai Records
Catalogue	BR93034
Country	Belgium
Year	1993
A1	The First Rebirth
B1	The Life Of Flow

JOSE AMNESIA
—The Eternal
Label	Eve Nova
Catalogue	EVENOVA005
Country	United Kingdom
Year	1999
A1	The Eternal (Original Mix)
B1	The Eternal (Life On Mars Remix)

JUNGLE HIGH WITH BLUE PEARL
—Fire Of Love
Label	Logic Records
Catalogue	LOC112
Country	United Kingdom
Year	1993
A1	Fire Of Love (Original Mix)
A2	Fire Of Love (Samurai Mix)
B1	Fire Of Love (Phil Perry Remix)
B2	Fire Of Love (Total Eclipse Mix)

JUNKIE XL
—B Y Whop To The Y/Siyncho
Label	Mostiko
Catalogue	R5086.6
Country	Belgium
Year	2001
A1	B Y Whop To The Y
B1	Siyncho

JUNO
—Eternal Love EP
Label	Adam & Eve Records
Catalogue	ADAM028
Country	Germany
Year	1995
A1	Eternal Love
B1	A Force Beyond
B2	Is It True?

JUNO REACTOR
—High Energy Protons
Label	NovaMute
Catalogue	12NoMu27
Country	United Kingdom
Year	1994
A1	High Energy Protons (Orion Mix)
B1	High Energy Protons (Voodoo People Mix)

JURGEN VRIES
—The Theme
Label	Direction Records
Catalogue	6730956
Country	United Kingdom
Year	2002
A1	The Theme (Original Mix)
B1	The Theme (JamX & De Leon's DuMonde Remix)

J.A.P.
—Burning Chrome
Label	303 Records
Catalogue	THREE02
Country	United Kingdom
Year	1994
A1	Burning Chrome
B1	Burning Chrome (Matrix Mix)

K

KAI TRACID
—Your Own Reality
Label	Suck Me Plasma
Catalogue	SUCK94
Country	Germany
Year	1997
A1	Your Own Reality (Energy Mix)
B1	Your Own Reality (Tracid Mix)
B2	Your Own Reality (Vocal Mix)

KAITO
—Soul of Heart
Label	Kompakt

Catalogue	KOM99
Country	Germany
Year	2004
A1	Soul Of Heart
B1	Peace Of Landscape

KAMAYA PAINTERS
—*Endless Wave*

Label	Data Records
Catalogue	DATA2
Country	United Kingdom
Year	1999
A1	Endless Wave (Original Mix)
B1	Endless Wave (Albion Remix)

KID VICIOUS
—*Re-Form*

Label	Tsunami
Catalogue	TSU6024
Country	Netherlands
Year	2000
A1	Re-Form (Original Mix)
B1	Re-Form (Tiësto remix)

KOLO
—*Track One*

Label	Fade Records
Catalogue	FD-011
Country	United States
Year	2000
A1	Track One (Kolo's Original Transmission)
B1	Track One (Steve Porter Remix)

KOMAKINO
—*Energy Trance EP*

Label	Suck Me Plasma
Catalogue	SUCK21
Country	Germany
Year	1993
A1	Outface (G60-Mix)
A2	Beyond Your Dreams
B1	Outface (Syncro Flash Remix)
B2	Beyond Your Dreams (Microbots Remix)

LANGE
—*I Believe*

Label	Additive
Catalogue	12AD039
Country	United Kingdom
Year	1999
A1	I Believe (Lange Mix)
B1	I Believe (DJ Tandu Remix)

LAZONBY
—*Sacred Cycles*

Label	Brainiak Records
Catalogue	BRAINK37
Country	United Kingdom
Year	1994
A1	Sacred Cycles
B1	The Charm

LEAMA
—*Requiem For A Dream*

Label	Perfecto
Catalogue	PERF048T
Country	United Kingdom
Year	2002
A1	Requiem For A Dream (Leama's Dream Mix)
B1	Requiem For A Dream (Leama's Ambient Mix)

LEGEND B.
—*Lost In Love*

Label	3 Lanka
Catalogue	3LAN006
Country	Germany
Year	1994
A1	Lost In Love (Sysex Style-Mix)
B1	Lost In Love (Spinclub-Mix)
B2	Love Seeds Passion (Gallery-Edit)

LELLO B. PRESENTS BLACK OUT VOL. 4
—*Sound Of Venus*

Label	Subway Records
Catalogue	SUB057
Country	Italy
Year	1994
A1	Sound Of Venus (Her Song Version)
A2	Sound Of Venus (Hypno Vibration Version)
B1	Sound Of Venus (Fastwind)
B2	Sound Of Venus (Bassline Time)

LEROY
—*The First Flight*

Label	Brainstorm
Catalogue	BRA015
Country	Italy
Year	1993
A1	The First Flight

LHASA
—*The Attic*

Label	Music Man Records
Catalogue	MMI9015
Country	Belgium
Year	1990
A1	The Attic
B1	Feel Dis Beat On
B2	Adhesive

LIAISONS D.
—*He Chilled Out*

Label	Logic Records
Catalogue	613383
Country	Germany
Year	1990
A1	He Chilled Out (Club Mix)
A2	He Chilled Out (Move Club Mix)
B1	Sirenas (Metronom Mix)

LIBRA PRESENTS TAYLOR
—*Anomaly/Calling Your Name*

Label	Platipus
Catalogue	PLAT24
Country	United Kingdom
Year	1996

A1	Anomaly—*Calling Your Name* (Granny's Epicure Mix)
B1	Anomaly—*Calling Your Name* (Forth's Remix)

LIGHTSCAPE
—*Inner-Warmth*
Label	Black Hole Recordings
Catalogue	BH168-5
Country	Netherlands
Year	2004
A1	Inner-Warmth (Original Mix)
B1	Inner-Warmth (Phynn's Overheated Remix)

LN MOVEMENT
—*Golden Desert*
Label	Illicit Cool Experiments
Catalogue	ICE901-5
Country	Netherlands
Year	2001
A1	Golden Desert Part 1
A2	Golden Desert Part 2
B1	Horizon
B2	Flooded Bridge

LNQ
—*People I Used To Know*
Label	Remark Records
Catalogue	RK007
Country	Netherlands
Year	2005
A1	People I Used To Know (Original Mix)
B1	People I Used To Know (Mike Foyle Remix)
B2	People I Used To Know (P.A. Groove Remix)

LOLO
—*Extended Horizon*
Label	Camouflage
Catalogue	CAM-2003-031
Country	Belgium
Year	2003
A1	Extended Horizon
B1	Landscape

LOOP CONTROL
—*Exceptionally Beautiful/Reflections*
Label	In Trance We Trust
Catalogue	ITWT308-5
Country	Netherlands
Year	1999
A1	Exceptionally Beautiful
B1	Reflections

LOOPHOLE
—*Deephole*
Label	Touché
Catalogue	TOU9518
Country	Netherlands
Year	1995
A1	Deephole
A2	Juzzfine
B1	Floating
B2	Soulsearch

LOST TRIBE
—*The Distant Voices EP*
Label	Hooj Choons
Catalogue	HOOJ54
Country	United Kingdom
Year	1997
A1	Angel
B1	Gamemaster

LOST WITNESS
—*7 Colours*
Label	Data Records
Catalogue	DATA15P1
Country	United Kingdom
Year	2000
A1	7 Colours (Angelic Remix)
B1	7 Colours (Original Mix)

LOVE INC
—*Trance Atlantic XS*
Label	Rising High Records
Catalogue	RSN43
Country	United Kingdom
Year	1992
A1	Dark Side Of The Moon
A2	Planetfall
B1	The Comeback
B2	Trance Atlantic XS

LUMINARY
—*My World*
Label	Lost Language
Catalogue	LOST046
Country	Netherlands
Year	2005
A1	My World (Original Mix)
B1	My World (Nikola Gala Mix)

LUSTRAL
—*Everytime*
Label	Hooj Choons
Catalogue	HOOJ55
Country	United Kingdom
Year	1997
A1	Everytime (Nalin & Kane Remix)
A2	Everytime (Red Jerry Mix)
B1	Everytime (Original Mix)

LUXOR
—*Superstitious*
Label	Lunatec
Catalogue	LUNA009
Country	Germany
Year	1994
A1	Superstitious (Nursery Mix)
B1	Superstitious (Dub Visions Mix)
B2	Superstitious (Club Heroes Remix)

LYRIC & NATALI
—*Over Emotion*
Label	Lost Language
Catalogue	LOST013
Country	United Kingdom
Year	2002
A1	Over Emotion (Spoiled Remix)
B1	Over Emotion (Smart System's Souvenir Mix)

L.S.G.
—Netherworld
Label	Hooj Choons
Catalogue	HOOJ52
Country	United Kingdom
Year	1997
A1	Netherworld (Vinyl Cut)
B1	Netherworld (Kid Loops Remix)

L-VEE
—Tears
Label	XTC
Catalogue	XTC038
Country	Belgium
Year	1999
A1	Tears
B1	Higher

M

MAJOR LEAGUE
—Wonder?/Wonder Where You Are?
Label	Captivating Sounds
Catalogue	CVS001
Country	Netherlands
Year	2000
A1	Wonder?
B1	Wonder Where You Are?

MANDALA
—High Noom EP
Label	Noom Records
Catalogue	NOOM005-6
Country	Germany
Year	1993
A1	The Encore
B1	Toray
B2	The Acid Of House

MAN WITH NO NAME
—Floor-Essence
Label	Perfecto FC
Catalogue	PERF108T
Country	United Kingdom
Year	1995
A1	Floor-Essence (Dayglo Mix)
B1	Floor-Essence (Black Light Mix)

MARC VISION
—Timegate
Label	Poison Recordings
Catalogue	POI-0019
Country	Germany
Year	1999
A1	Time Gate (Update)
B1	Time Gate (Original)
B2	The Shark

MARC 'N' ACE
—Conquest Paradise
Label	Scuba Records
Catalogue	SCUBA003
Country	Germany
Year	1999
A1	Dark Priest
B1	Conquest Paradise

MARCO V
—Simulated
Label	ID&T
Catalogue	7004435
Country	Netherlands
Year	2001
A1	Simulated (Original Mix)
B1	Simulated (Marco's V.ision Remix)

MARCOS & JK WALKER
—Apache 7
Label	Active Media
Catalogue	ACM009
Country	United Kingdom
Year	2004
A1	Apache 7 (Marcos Mix)
B1	Apache 7 (JK Walker Mix)

MARIO PIÙ AKA DJ ARABESQUE
—The Vision
Label	BXR
Catalogue	BXR1101
Country	Italy
Year	2000
A1	The Vision (Vision 1 Mix)
B1	The Vision (Vision 2 Mix)
B2	Bass Control

MARK NORMAN
—Return 2 Eden/Overkill
Label	Silver Premium
Catalogue	SP-050
Country	Netherlands
Year	2001
A1	Return 2 Eden
B1	Overkill

MARK OTTEN
—Mushroom Therapy
Label	Armind
Catalogue	ARMD1004
Country	Netherlands
Year	2003
A1	Mushroom Therapy (Lightscape Mix)
B1	Mushroom Therapy (Armin van Buuren Remix)

Markus Schulz presents Elevation
—Clear Blue
Label	Electronic Elements
Catalogue	ELEL001
Country	Netherlands
Year	2004
A1	Clear Blue (Original Mix)
B1	Clear Blue (Intro Mix)

MARMION
—Schöneberg
Label	Urban
Catalogue	None
Country	Germany
Year	1994
A1	Schöneberg (Original Mix)
B1	Schöneberg (Marmion Remix)
B2	Schöneberg (Kid Paul Remix)

MARVO GENETIC
—New World Basics
Label	Deviate
Catalogue	DV8-004
Country	Netherlands
Year	1993
A1	The Fourth Wave (Original Mix)
B1	The Fourth Wave (Vocal Mix)
B2	The Opposite Wave

MATANKA
—Lost In A Dream
Label	Camouflage
Catalogue	CM-2001-015
Country	Belgium
Year	2001
A1	Lost In A Dream (Marco Zaffarano Remix)
B1	Lost In A Dream (DJ Tandu Remix)
B2	Lost In A Dream (Original Mix)

MAURO PICOTTO
—Lizard
Label	BXR
Catalogue	BXR1048
Country	Italy
Year	1998
A1	Lizard (Picotto Mix)
A2	Lizard (Tea Mix)
B1	Lizard (Mondo Bongo Mix)
B2	Lizard (Nation Mix)

MAX GRAHAM
—Falling Together
Label	Hope Recordings
Catalogue	HOPE022
Country	United Kingdom
Year	2001
A1	Falling Together
B1	Shoreline (Club Mix)

MEDWAY
—The Resurrection EP
Label	Hooj Choons
Catalogue	HOOJ66
Country	United Kingdom
Year	1998
A1	Resurrection
B1	Vibrations (Dub Mix)
B2	Slow Resurrection

MEMBERS OF MAYDAY
—Sonic Empire
Label	Low Spirit Recordings
Catalogue	74321475301
Country	Germany
Year	1997
A1	Sonic Empire
B1	Easy Over

MERIDIAN
—Reach For The Stars
Label	Green Martian
Catalogue	GM2000-027
Country	Belgium
Year	2000
A1	Reach For The Stars
B1	Area 99

MESH
—Purple Haze
Label	In Trance We Trust
Catalogue	ITWT349-5
Country	Netherlands
Year	2003
A1	Purple Haze
B1	Esthetic Visions

METAL MASTER
—Vol. 1
Label	Harthouse
Catalogue	HH-002
Country	Germany
Year	1992
A1	Simply Metal
B1	Spectrum

MICROGLOBE
—High On Hope
Label	MFS
Catalogue	MFS7019-0
Country	Germany
Year	1992
A1	High On Hope (Technooligan Edit)
B1	High On Hope (Twisted Version)
B2	High On Hope (Micro Beats)

MIDI NETWORK/SNOWDOME
—Twisted Systems Vol. 1
Label	Abfahrt Records
Catalogue	AR001
Country	United Kingdom
Year	1994
A1	Midi Network—Heaven & Hell
B1	Snowdome—Murdoch Most Foul (One Way System Remix)
B2	Snowdome—Murdoch Most Foul (Original Mix)

MIDWAY
—Monkey Forest
Label	In Trance We Trust
Catalogue	ITWT333-5
Country	Netherlands
Year	2002
A1	Monkey Forest
B1	Travelling

MIKE FOYLE VS. SIGNALRUNNERS
—Love Theme Dusk
Label	Armind
Catalogue	ARMD1018
Country	Netherlands
Year	2005
A1	Love Theme Dusk (Mike's Broken Record Mix)
B1	Love Theme Dusk (Signalrunners Sunrise Mix)
B2	Love Theme Dusk (Airbase presents Parc Remix)

MINIMALISTIX
—Close Cover
Label	Data Records

Catalogue	DATA32T
Country	United Kingdom
Year	2002
A1	Close Cover (Original Mix)
B1	Close Cover (Boss@Nova Remix)

MIRAGE
—Airborn
Label	Eye Q Records
Catalogue	EYEQ008
Country	Germany
Year	1993
A1	Airborn
B1	Airborn (O-Mix)
B2	Airborn (G-Mix)

MIRO FEATURING EDDIE
—Celebrate
Label	Effective Records
Catalogue	EFFS010
Country	United Kingdom
Year	1993
A1	Celebrate (Vocal Mix)
B1	Cocoon (Original Mix)
B2	Celebrate (Dub)

MISS SHIVA
—Dreams
Label	Dance Division
Catalogue	DAD6683206
Country	Germany
Year	1999
A1	Dreams (Sunbeam Mix)
B1	Dream (Shiva's Club Cut)

MOBY
—Go
Label	Outer Rhythm
Catalogue	FOOT15
Country	United Kingdom
Year	1991
A1	Go (Woodtick Mix)
B1	Go (Low Spirit Mix)
B2	Go (Voodoo Child Mix)

MOOGWAI
—Viola
Label	Platipus
Catalogue	PLAT71
Country	United Kingdom
Year	2000
A1	Viola (Original Mix)
B1	Viola (Armin van Buuren Remix)

MOONMAN
—Galaxia
Label	Go For It
Catalogue	GO9609
Country	Germany
Year	1996
A1	Galaxia (Original Mix)
B1	Galaxia (DJ Errik Remix)
B2	Marsfire

MORGAN WILD PROJECT
—Submersion/Analog Flash
Label	Buzz
Catalogue	BZZXL106601
Country	Belgium
Year	1992
A1	Submersion
A2	Submersion Beats
B1	Analog Flash
B2	Trance Mission

MOTORCYCLE
—As The Rush Comes
Label	Armind
Catalogue	ARMD1001
Country	Netherlands
Year	2003
A1	As The Rush Comes (Gabriel & Dresden Sweeping Strings Mix)
B1	As The Rush Comes (Armin van Buuren's Universal Religion Mix)

MRE
—The Deep Edge
Label	Le Petit Prince
Catalogue	PRIN9971-6
Country	Germany
Year	1999
A1	The Deep Edge
B1	Sectors One And Two
B2	Footprints

MR. SAM VS. FRED BAKER PRESENT AS ONE
—Forever Waiting
Label	Magik Muzik
Catalogue	MM809-5
Country	Netherlands
Year	2003
A1	Forever Waiting (Original Mix)
B1	Forever Waiting (M.I.K.E. Remix)

MYSTICA
—African Horizon
Label	Perfecto
Catalogue	SAM3196
Country	United Kingdom
Year	1998
A1	African Horizon (Mystica Mix)
B1	Bliss (Mystica Mix)
C1	African Horizon (X-Cabs Remix 1)
D1	African Horizon (X-Cabs Remix 2)

MYSTIC FORCE
—Psychic Harmony
Label	MFS
Catalogue	123.7060.0
Country	Germany
Year	1994
A1	Mystic Force
A2	Clearlight
B1	Mystic Force (Psychic Harmony Remix)

M.I.K.E.
—Sunrise At Palamos
Label	XTC
Catalogue	XTC055
Country	Belgium

Year	2000
A1	Sunrise At Palamos
B1	Someone Somewhere

M.O.R.P.H.
—Consequence
Label	ID&T
Catalogue	7005215
Country	Netherlands
Year	2002
A1	Consequence (Benicio Remix)
B1	Consequence (Woody van Eyden Remix)
B2	Consequence (Original Mix)

N

NAGHACHIAN II
—Down
Label	Frankfurt Beat Productions
Catalogue	901023.6
Country	Germany
Year	1994
A1	Down (Survival Edit)
B1	On 'Da Landing Platform
B2	Again

NALIN & KANE
—Beachball
Label	Full Frequency Range Recordings
Catalogue	567831-1
Country	United Kingdom
Year	1997
A1	Beachball (Tall Paul Remix)
B1	Beachball (Original Club Mix)

NEUTRON 9000 VS. THE MYSTERIES OF SCIENCE
—Tranceplant/Open Your Mind
Label	MFS
Catalogue	MFS0700015
Country	Germany
Year	1992
A1	Tranceplant
B1	Open Your Mind

NEVER
—Singe
Label	Important Records
Catalogue	IMP016
Country	Germany
Year	1995
A1	Singe
B1	Dripping Blue
B2	Hellbent

NEXUS 6
—Trés Chic EP
Label	Noom Records
Catalogue	NOOM006-12
Country	Germany
Year	1994
A1	Trés Chic
B1	Time Chic
B2	AB-Chic

NICKELSON
—Aquaphonic
Label	Karma
Catalogue	KARMA1003-5
Country	Netherlands
Year	1998
A1	Aquaphonic (Original)
B1	Aquaphonic (DJ Tiësto & DJ Jim Remix)
B2	Aquaphonic (Edit)

NO KEY—GOODBYE
—It's A Small Country
Label	Abfahrt Records
Catalogue	ABF0017-12
Country	Germany
Year	1993
A1	It's A Small Country
B1	MKS—Kick (Hierbas Mix)

NOCTURNAL HIGH
—Let'em Hear/Dreamstate
Label	Nocturnal High
Catalogue	NOCT002
Country	United Kingdom
Year	1995
A1	Let'em Hear
B1	Dreamstate

NOSTRUM
—Brainchild
Label	Pull The Strings
Catalogue	PTS009-6
Country	United Kingdom
Year	1996
A1	Brainchild (Original)
B1	Brainchild (DJ Tom And Norman Mix)
B2	Brainchild (Acid Mix)

NOVA NOVA
—Ex-EP
Label	F Communications
Catalogue	F037
Country	France
Year	1996
A1	U
A2	Tones (Ibid)
B1	Ex-El-Echo
B2	See

NU NRG
—Dreamland
Label	Vandit Records
Catalogue	VANDIT012
Country	Germany
Year	2002
A1	Dreamland (Rank 1 Re-Edit)
B1	Dreamland (Original Mix)

O

OCEANLAB FEATURING JUSTINE SUISSA
—Clear Blue Water
Label	Club Culture
Catalogue	092744468-0
Country	Germany

Year	2002
A1	Clear Blue Water (Hennes & Cold Club Remix)
A2	Clear Blue Water (Above & Beyond Progressive Remix)
B1	Clear Blue Water (Original Mix)
B2	Clear Blue Water (Ferry Corsten Remix)

OLIVER KLEIN
—Rheinkraft

Label	B-Sides
Catalogue	BSI013
Country	Germany
Year	2000
A1	Rheinkraft
B1	Plexiglas

OLIVER LIEB
—Subraumstimulation

Label	Orbit Records
Catalogue	DMDORBIT030
Country	Germany
Year	1999
A1	Subraumstimulation (Main Mix)
B1	Subraumstimulation (Johnson Mix)
B2	Subraumstimulation (W.J. Henze Mix)

OM
—Instant Enlightenment

Label	C&S Records
Catalogue	CS2011
Country	United States
Year	1994
A1	Physical Reality
B1	Seed Of Sound
B2	Wheels Of Light

ONGAKU
—Mihon

Label	Pod Communication
Catalogue	POD026
Country	Germany
Year	1992
A1	Mihon #1
A2	Mihon #2
B1	Mihon #3

ORBITAL
—Halcyon

Label	Full Frequency Range Recordings
Catalogue	162350009-1
Country	United States
Year	1992
A1	Halcyon
B1	The Naked And The Dub

ORBITAL VELOCITY
—Last Voyage

Label	Foresight Records
Catalogue	FSR003
Country	Germany
Year	1998
A1	Last Voyage (Paramount Park-Mix)
B1	Last Voyage (Club Mix)

ORIGIN
—Wide-Eyed Angel

Label	Steel Yard Music
Catalogue	SYW004
Country	United Kingdom
Year	1999
A1	Wide-Eyed Angel (Inversion Mix)
B1	Wide-Eyed Angel (Exposed Mix)

ORKIDEA
—Unity

Label	Steel Fish Blue
Catalogue	SFB001
Country	United Kingdom
Year	1999
A1	Unity

O.V.N.I.
—Soundspore/Neology

Label	POF Music
Catalogue	458002630
Country	France
Year	1996
A1	Soundspore
B1	Neology (Nu Mix)

P

PABLO GARGANO
—Eve 1

Label	Eve Records
Catalogue	EVE9501
Country	United Kingdom
Year	1995
A1	Pink Fluyd
B1	Graceland
B2	Juggernaut On The M25

PARAGLIDERS
—Paragliders EP

Label	Superstition
Catalogue	SUPERSTITION2012
Country	Germany
Year	1993
A1	Paraglide (Original Mix)
A2	Bagdad
B1	Paraglide (Blue Sky Mix)

PAUL OAKENFOLD
—Southern Sun/Ready Steady Go

Label	Perfecto
Catalogue	PERF017T
Country	United Kingdom
Year	2002
A1	Southern Sun (Original Mix)
B1	Ready Steady Go
B2	Southern Sun (Sabata Breaks Vocal Mix)
C1	Southern Sun (DJ Tiësto Mix)
D1	Southern Sun (Gabriel & Dresden Mix)

PAUL VAN DYK
—45 RPM
(The Special Spanish EP Version)

Label	Max Music
Catalogue	NM1072EP

Country	Spain
Year	1994
A1	For An Angel
A2	I'm Comin' (To Take You Away Too)
B1	45 RPM
B2	Pump This On 45
B3	A Magical Moment

PERPETUOUS DREAMER
—The Sound Of Goodbye
Label	Armind
Catalogue	ARMD1007
Country	Netherlands
Year	2001
A1	The Sound Of Goodbye (Armin's Tribal Feel)
B1	The Sound Of Goodbye (Armin Van Buuren's Rising Star Mix)

PERRY & RHODAN
—The Beat Just Goes Straight On & On
Label	Rising High Records
Catalogue	RSN70
Country	United Kingdom
Year	1993
A1	The Beat Just Goes Straight On & On (Straight On & On & On & On & On Mix)
A2	The Beat Just Goes Straight On & On (Beat Mix)
B1	Voice Box
B2	The Beat Just Goes Straight On & On (Perry & Rhodan's Version)
B3	The Beat Just Goes Straight On &On (All The Time Mix)

PETER MARTIN PRESENTS ANTHANASIA
—Perfect Wave
Label	Electronic Elements
Catalogue	ELEL003
Country	Netherlands
Year	2004
A1	Perfect Wave (Original Mix)
B1	Perfect Wave (Oahu Break Dub)

PEYOTE
—Alcatraz
Label	R&S Records
Catalogue	RS92033
Country	Belgium
Year	1992
A1	Alcatraz
B1	I Will Fight No More

PHANTASIA
—Violet Skies
Label	Mental Radio
Catalogue	MR005
Country	Belgium
Year	1991
A1	Violet Skies
B1	Violet Skies (A Capella)
B2	Violet Skies (Instrumental)

PHD
—Summer Storm
Label	Foreign Policy
Catalogue	FP12002
Country	United Kingdom
Year	1994
A1	Summer Storm (Earth Needs Rain Mix)
B1	Summer Storm (Leisure Lounge Edit)

PHYNN
—Lucid
Label	In Trance We Trust
Catalogue	ITWT376-5
Country	Netherlands
Year	2005
A1	Lucid
B1	Solitude

PJ
—Elysium
Label	Stickman Records
Catalogue	STIK027
Country	Canada
Year	1995
A1	Elysium
A2	Elysian Fields
B1	Vibes
B2	Dancing Keys

PLANET PERFECTO
—Bullet In The Gun
Label	Perfecto
Catalogue	PERF3T
Country	United Kingdom
Year	1999
A1	Bullet In The Gun (Saturday Mix)
B1	Bullet In The Gun (Mekka vs Trouser Enthusiasts)

PLANISPHERE
—O
Label	Green Martian
Catalogue	GM99023
Country	Belgium
Year	1999
A1	O
B1	So Many Ways

PLASTIC BOY
—Twixt
Label	Bonzai Trance Progressive
Catalogue	BTP4898
Country	Belgium
Year	1998
A1	Twixt
B1	Life Isn't Easy

PLEIADIANS
—Pleiadians/Boarding Pass To Balangan
Label	Symbiosis Records
Catalogue	SYMB009
Country	United Kingdom
Year	1995
A1	Pleiadians
B1	Boarding Pass To Balangan

POB

−*Boiler/Beast*
Label	Seismic Records
Catalogue	SMC009
Country	United Kingdom
Year	1997
A1	Boiler
B1	Beast

POLE FOLDER & CP
−*Apollo Vibes*
Label	Bedrock Records
Catalogue	BED19
Country	United Kingdom
Year	2001
A1	Apollo Vibes
B1	Apollo Vibes (Young American Primitive's Spacecraft Communicator Mix)

POLTERGEIST
−*Vicious Circles*
Label	Platipus
Catalogue	PLAT02
Country	United Kingdom
Year	1993
A1	Vicious Circles (Spirit Level Mix)
B1	Vicious Circles (Magic Circle Mix)
B2	Vicious Circles (Catalyst Remix)

POSITIVE THINKING
−*Infinite*
Label	MFS
Catalogue	123.7054.0.18
Country	Germany
Year	1994
A1	Infinite (Future)
A2	Compression
B1	Morris
B2	Infinite Orbit

PPK
−*ResuRection*
Label	Perfecto
Catalogue	PERF32T
Country	United Kingdom
Year	2001
A1	ResuRection (Space Club Mix)
B1	ResuRection (Wellenrausch Remix)
B2	Robots Outro

PQM
−*You Are Sleeping*
Label	Yoshitoshi Recordings
Catalogue	YR104
Country	United States
Year	2003
A1	You Are Sleeping (Dave From Dallas & DJ Redeye Dub Mix)
A2	You Are Sleeping (Acapella)
B1	You Are Sleeping (PQM's Meet Luke Chable Vocal Pass)
C1	You Are Sleeping (PQM's Meet Luke Chable Dub Pass)
D1	You Are Sleeping (Dave From Dallas & DJ Redeye Vocal Mix)

PSYCHAOS
−*Science Fiction/They Tried To Grab Me*
Label	Blue Room Released
Catalogue	BR007
Country	United Kingdom
Year	1995
A1	Science Fiction
B1	They Tried To Grab Me

PSYCHICK WARRIORS OV GAIA
−*Exit 23*
Label	KK Records
Catalogue	KK055
Country	Belgium
Year	1990
A1	Exit 23 (Source)
B1	Exit 23 (Return)

PULSATION
−*Pulsation*
Label	Harthouse
Catalogue	HH011
Country	Germany
Year	1992
A1	It's So Simple To Do
B1	Transpulsation
B2	Pulsar

PULSER
−*Cloudwalking*
Label	A Trance Communication Release
Catalogue	TCOM005
Country	United Kingdom
Year	1999
A1	Cloudwalking (Original Mix)
B1	Cloudwalking (Astral Mix)

PUSH
−*The Real Anthem*
Label	Bonzai Records
Catalogue	BR98137
Country	Belgium
Year	1998
A1	Universal Nation
B1	Prisma

P.O.S.
−*Gravity*
Label	Anjunabeats
Catalogue	ANJ-039
Country	United Kingdom
Year	2005
A1	Gravity (Original Mix)
B1	Gravity (Arksun's Voyage Mix)

Q

QUADRAN
−*Eternally*
Label	Bonzai Trance Progressive
Catalogue	BTP0195
Country	Belgium
Year	1995
A1	Eternally (Dance Mix)

A2	Eternally (Single Edit)
B1	The Walker

QUAZAR
—Sunflower
Label	Seven Stars Records
Catalogue	STAR005
Country	Netherlands
Year	1994
A1	Sunflower
B1	Moonflower
B2	Starflower

QUENCH
—Dreams
Label	Infectious Records
Catalogue	INFECT3
Country	United Kingdom
Year	1993
A1	Dreams (Extended Mix)
A2	Dreams (Radio Edit)
B1	Dreams (Crunched Up Mix)
B2	Dreams (Crunched Down Mix)

QUIETMAN
—The Sleeper
Label	Platipus
Catalogue	PLAT37
Country	United kingdom
Year	1998
A1	The Sleeper
B1	The Sleeper (Man With No Name Remix)

QUIVVER
—She Does
Label	VC Recordings
Catalogue	VCRT61
Country	United Kingdom
Year	2000
A1	She Does (Quivver Mix)
B1	She Does (Quivver's Alternative Mix)

R

RABBIT IN THE MOON
—Phases Of An Out-Of-Body Experience
Label	Hardkiss
Catalogue	HK005
Country	United States
Year	1994
A1	Phase 1—First Contact
A2	Phase 3—Burning Spear
B1	Phase 5—Enlightenment
B2	Phase 7—Original
B3	Phase 9—Lunar Eclipse

RAIN FOREST
—The Birds
Label	Rain Forest Records
Catalogue	RF3
Country	United Kingdom
Year	1993
A1	The Birds (Deep Trance Mix)
B1	Rising (Euro Mix)

RALPHIE B
—Massive
Label	Vandit Records
Catalogue	VANDIT017
Country	Germany
Year	2002
A1	Massive (Original Mix)
B1	Massive (Filterheadz Remix)
C1	Massive (Mirco De Govia Mix)
D1	Disclosure

RAMIN
—Vol. II: Brainticket
Label	Logic Records
Catalogue	LUK008
Country	United Kingdom
Year	1992
A1	Brainticket (Remix)
B1	Brainticket (Original)

RANDY KATANA
—In Silence
Label	Reset Records
Catalogue	RS005
Country	Netherlands
Year	2004
A1	In Silence (Txitxarro Mix)
B1	In Silence (Scratch Bandicoot Remix)

RANK 1
—Airwave
Label	Free For All
Catalogue	7002725
Country	Netherlands
Year	1999
A1	Airwave (Original Mix)
B1	Airwave (Rank 1 vs. Dutch Force Remix)

RAPID EYE
—Circa-Forever
Label	A Trance Communication Release
Catalogue	TCOM019
Country	United Kingdom
Year	2002
A1	Circa-Forever (Iberia's Main Room Mix)
B1	Circa-Forever (Rapid Eye's R.E.mix)

READY FOR DEAD
—Ready For Dead
Label	Limbo Records
Catalogue	LIMB014T
Country	United Kingdom
Year	1993
A1	Ready For Dead
B1	Ready For Dead (Ambient Mix)

RED SUN
—This Love
Label	Hooj Choons

Catalogue	HOOJ49
Country	United Kingdom
Year	1996
A1	This Love (Longredsun Mix)
B1	This Love (Our House Remix)

REEL X
−Feels Good
Label	Influence Recordings
Catalogue	IR020-12
Country	Germany
Year	1994
A1	Feels Good (Original Mix)
B1	Feels Good (Remix)
B2	Trip Into Your Body

REFLEKT FEATURING DELLINE BASS
−Need To Feel Loved
Label	Positiva
Catalogue	12TIVDJ213
Country	United Kingdom
Year	2004
A1	Need To Feel Loved (12" Club Mix)
B1	Need To Feel Loved (The Thrillseekers Remix)

RENEGADE LEGION
−Friends Or Foes?
Label	Fnac Music Dance Division
Catalogue	590279
Country	France
Year	1993
A1	Friends Or Foes?
B1	The Weeping Waste
B2	The Renegade March

RESISTANCE D
−Cosmic Love
Label	Cyclotron
Catalogue	LEPTONE16
Country	Germany
Year	1991
A1	Cosmic Love
B1	Index (Mix 1)
B2	Index (Mix 2)

REXANTHONY
−Polaris Dream
Label	S.O.B. (Sound Of The Bomb)
Catalogue	SOB244
Country	Italy
Year	1995
A1	Polaris Dream (Radio Version)
B1	Polaris Dream (Hardacid Version)
B2	Polaris Dream (Club Version)

RE: LOCATE
−Waterfall
Label	Galactive
Catalogue	GALSO003
Country	Netherlands
Year	2003
A1	Waterfall
B1	Passion

RIDGEWALKERS FEATURING EL
−Find
Label	Baroque Records
Catalogue	BARQ039
Country	United Kingdom
Year	2004
A1	Find (Andy Moor Remix)
B1	Find (Original Mix)

RIVA
−Stringer
Label	Alien Recordings
Catalogue	ALIEN021
Country	Netherlands
Year	2001
A1	Stringer
B1	Mistral

RMB
−Spring
Label	Low Spirit Recordings
Catalogue	576665-1
Country	Germany
Year	1996
A1	Spring (Vocal Mix)
A2	Spring (Straight Mix)
B1	Whispering

ROBERT GITELMAN
−Things 2 Say
Label	ID&T
Catalogue	7006525
Country	Netherlands
Year	2003
A1	Things 2 Say (Original Mix)
B1	Things 2 Say (M.I.K.E. Remix)

ROBERT MILES
−Children
Label	DBX Records
Catalogue	DBX015
Country	Italy
Year	1995
A1	Children (Dream Version)
B1	Children (Original Version)
B2	Children (Message Version)

ROBERT NICKSON
−Spiral
Label	A State Of Trance
Catalogue	ASOT015
Country	Netherlands
Year	2004
A1	Spiral (Original Mix)
B1	Spiral (MK-S Remix)
B2	Spiral (Alucard's Star Ocean Mix)

ROLAND BRANT
−Moon's Waterfalls
Label	Désastre Records
Catalogue	DES9601
Country	Italy
Year	1996

A1	Moon's Waterfalls (Dream Version)
B1	Moon's Waterfalls (Progressive Version)

ROLAND KLINKENBERG
—Inner Laugh
Label	Sim
Catalogue	SIM11
Country	Netherlands
Year	1998
A1	Inner Laugh
A2	Illuminated
B1	Reprise
B2	Earth Reversion

RON VAN DEN BEUKEN
—Timeless
Label	Liquid Recordings
Catalogue	LQ034
Country	Netherlands
Year	2003
A1	Timeless (Ron Van Den Beuken Remix)
B1	Timeless (Original Mix)

RUI DA SILVA
—Touch Me
Label	Kismet
Catalogue	KMT004
Country	United Kingdom
Year	2000
A1	Touch Me (Original Mix)
B1	Touch Me (Saffron Mix)

RUSS GABRIEL
—Digilogic Synthesis EP
Label	Force Inc. Music Works
Catalogue	FIMVS1
Country	Germany
Year	1994
A1	Digilogic
A2	Mindseeker
B1	Unit Prefix
B2	Virgin Birth

R.A.F. BY PICOTTO
—Ocean Whispers
Label	GFB Records
Catalogue	GFB092
Country	Italy
Year	1996
A1	Ocean Whispers (R.A.F. Zone Mix)
B1	Ocean Whispers (Planet Mix)
B2	Ocean Whispers (Dream House Mix)

R.D.1
—Total Eclipse EP
Label	Rising High Records
Catalogue	RSN59
Country	United Kingdom
Year	1993
A1	Eclipse (DSL Remix)
B1	Eclipse
B2	Cut-Off

R.O.O.S.
—Instant Moments
Label	Basic Beat Recordings
Catalogue	BASIC253-5
Country	Netherlands
Year	1997
A1	Instant Moments (Moederoverste Onie Mix)
B1	Instant Moments (Original Mix)
B2	Instant Moments (Dance Therapy Mix)

S

SACCOMAN
—Pyramid Soundwave
Label	BXR
Catalogue	BXR1008
Country	Italy
Year	1996
A1	Sunshine Dance
A2	A Piece Of Trance
B1	Pyramid Soundwave

SAINTS & SINNERS
—Pushin Too Hard
Label	Sounds Good Records
Catalogue	SGR018
Country	Germany
Year	1999
A1	Pushin Too Hard
B1	Dub Trump

SAKIN & FRIENDS
—Protect Your Mind
Label	Planet Love Records
Catalogue	PLO010-6
Country	Germany
Year	1997
A1	Protect Your Mind
B1	Protect Yourself

SALT TANK
—ST 6 Eugina
Label	Internal
Catalogue	LIARX29
Country	United Kingdom
Year	1996
A1	Eugina (Pacific Diva)
B1	Eugina (Charged Up)
B2	Eugina (Sargasso Sea)

SALTWATER
—The Legacy
Label	Zenith Records
Catalogue	ZEN3001
Country	Germany
Year	2003
A1	The Legacy (Alphazone Mix)
B1	The Legacy (Club Mix)

SANDER KLEINENBERG
—My Lexicon
Label	Essential Recordings
Catalogue	ESX16
Country	United Kingdom
Year	2000

A1	My Lexicon (Full Length Version)
B1	My Lexicon (12" Version)
B2	Storm

SASHA
−Xpander
Label	Deconstruction
Catalogue	74321681991
Country	United Kingdom
Year	1999
A1	Xpander
B1	Belfunk
C1	Rabbitweed
D1	Baja

SCHILLER
−Das Glockenspiel
Label	What's Up?!
Catalogue	567865-1
Country	Germany
Year	1998
A1	Das Glockenspiel (X/tended)
B1	Das Glockenspiel (Free Schiller Mix)
B2	Das Glockenspiel (Video Edit)

SECOND SUN
−Empire
Label	Vandit Records
Catalogue	VANDIT016
Country	Germany
Year	2002
A1	Empire (Original Mix)
A2	The Answer
B1	Empire (TPOD Mix by Paul van Dyk)

SENSENET
−Sushi EP
Label	Uptown
Catalogue	UPTOWN501
Country	Germany
Year	1994
A1	Sushi I
A2	X-Oniq
B1	Sushi II
B2	Waiting Zone
B3	Circle 5

SENSORIA
−Run 4 Love
Label	Dance Pollution
Catalogue	POLL001
Country	Italy
Year	1995
A1	Run 4 Love (Nagoya)
A2	Run 4 Love (Mioshi)
B1	Run 4 Love (Kobe)
B2	Run 4 Love (Sendai)

SEOFON
−Access EP
Label	Visible Records
Catalogue	VIS-103
Country	United States
Year	1994
A1	Scharæ

A2	The Joyning
B1	Paseq
B2	Ylem

SHAKTA
−Cosmic Trigger/Spiritual Beings In Physical Bodies
Label	Dragonfly Records
Catalogue	BFLT41
Country	United Kingdom
Year	1997
A1	Cosmic Trigger
B1	Spiritual Beings In Physical Bodies

SHANE
−Too Late To Turn/Toujours
Label	Sphear
Catalogue	23200706
Country	Belgium
Year	2000
A1	Too Late To Turn
B1	Toujours

SIDDHARTHA
−De La Trance
Label	Millennium Records
Catalogue	MILL12-003
Country	Germany
Year	1994
A1	De La Trance ('Headman' Mix)
B1	New Coming
B2	De La Trance

SIGNUM
−First Strike
Label	Jinx Records
Catalogue	JX-660
Country	Netherlands
Year	2001
A1	First Strike
B1	In Progress

SOLAR FACTOR
−No Return
Label	Platipus Euro
Catalogue	EPLAT001
Country	United Kingdom
Year	2003
A1	No Return (Original Mix)
B1	No Return (Neo & Farina Mix)

SOLAR QUEST
−Into The Machine
Label	Choci's Chewns
Catalogue	CC005
Country	United Kingdom
Year	1994
A1	Into The Machine
B1	Acid Eye Full

SOLAR STONE
−Seven Cities
Label	Hooj Choons
Catalogue	HOOJ85F
Country	United Kingdom
Year	1999
A1	Seven Cities (Solar Stone's

	Atlantis Mix)
B1	Seven Cities (V-One's 'Living Cities' Remix)

SOLID GLOBE
—Global Demand EP
Label	Fundamental Recordings
Catalogue	FUNLTDEP001
Country	Netherlands
Year	2004
A1	North Pole
B1	Sahara

SOLID SESSIONS
—Janeiro
Label	Combined Forces
Catalogue	CF026
Country	Netherlands
Year	2000
A1	Janeiro (Original Mix)
B1	Janeiro (Harry Lemon Remix)

SONIC INC.
—Taste Of Summer
Label	Space Traxx
Catalogue	SPAX032
Country	Germany
Year	2000
A1	Taste Of Summer
B1	Look Into My Mind

SONIC INFUSION
—Magnifica
Label	Eye Q Records
Catalogue	EYEQ006
Country	Germany
Year	1992
A1	Magnifica (Original Mix)
B1	Magnifica (Break-Beat-Mix)
B2	Unfuture

SOURMASH
—Pilgramage To Paradise
Label	Prolekult
Catalogue	KULT001
Country	United Kingdom
Year	1993
A1	Pilgramage To Paradise (Barrel Beat Mix)
B1	Pilgramage To Paradise (Paradise Club Mix)

SPACEBUGGY
—Spacebuggy EP
Label	Out On A Limb
Catalogue	OOL2T
Country	United Kingdom
Year	1994
A1	Spacebuggy
A2	Spacebuggy
B1	Spacebuggy

SPACE MANOEUVRES
—Stage One
Label	Hooj Choons
Catalogue	HOOJ79
Country	United Kingdom
Year	2000
A1	Stage One (Space Manoeuvre's Separation Mix)
B1	Stage One (Tilt's Apollo 11 Mix)

SPECT-R
—Spaceride
Label	Monokultur
Catalogue	MONO0003
Country	Germany
Year	1995
A1	Enjoy Your Spaceride
B1	Hardride

SPICELAB
—Quicksand EP
Label	Harthouse
Catalogue	HH010
Country	Germany
Year	1992
A1	Quicksand
B1	Amorph
B2	56387

STAMINA
—Polaris EP
Label	Global AMBition
Catalogue	GAMB005-6
Country	Germany
Year	1994
A1	Polaris (Part 1)
A2	Polaris (Part 2)
B1	Stranded Selen
B2	Hatari

STARECASE
—Faith
Label	Hope Recordings
Catalogue	HOPE031
Country	United Kingdom
Year	2002
A1	Faith (Original)
B1	Faith (Loafer Mix)

STATE OF GRACE
—Not Over Yet
Label	Perfecto
Catalogue	PERF1T
Country	United Kingdom
Year	1993
A1	Not Over Yet (Perfecto Mix)
B1	Not Over Yet (Trance Mix)
B2	Not Over Yet (State Of Grace Mix)

STEF
—Sound Family EP
Label	Sadie Records
Catalogue	SADIE002
Country	United Kingdom
Year	1999
A1	Joachim
B1	Steffan
B2	Marvin

STRAY DOG
—Mirror

Label	Black Hole Recordings
Catalogue	BH111-5
Country	Netherlands
Year	1999
A1	Mirror (Signum Remix)
B1	Mirror (HH's Convex Mix)
B2	Mirror (Original Mix)

SULTAN & THE GREEK
—Rezin b/w Wadi

Label	Shinichi
Catalogue	SHI027
Country	United States
Year	2004
A1	Wadi (Dub Mix)
B1	Rezin (Original Mix)
C1	Rezin (Valentino Mix)
D1	Wadi (Vocal Mix)

SUNBEAM
—Outside World EP

Label	Suck Me Plasma
Catalogue	SUCK27
Country	Germany
Year	1994
A1	Outside World
B1	La Musique (C'est Notre Drogue)
B2	Smoke

SUNBURST
—Eyeball (Eyeball Paul's Theme)

Label	Virgin
Catalogue	VTST4
Country	United Kingdom
Year	2000
A1	Eyeball (Eyeball Paul's Theme) (Original Mix)
A2	Eyeball (Eyeball Paul's Theme) (John Johnson Remix 12" Edit)
B1	Eyeball (Eyeball Paul's Theme) (Pulser Remix 12" Edit)

SUNTORY
—Cybernetic Voyager

Label	Désastre Records
Catalogue	DES9525
Country	Italy
Year	1995
A1	Cybernetic Voyager (Original Mix)
A2	Cybernetic Voyager (Version One)
B1	Cybernetic Voyager (Version Two)
B2	Cybernetic Voyager (Version Three)

SVEN VÄTH
—Ritual Of Life (Ritual Mixes)

Label	Eye Q Records
Catalogue	4509-92100-0
Country	Germany
Year	1993
A1	Ritual Of Life (The Tribal Acid Mix)
B1	Ritual Of Life (Breakbeat Mix)
B2	Ritual Of Life (Neutron 9000 Mix)

SVENSON + GIELEN
—The Beauty Of Silence

Label	ID&T
Catalogue	7003465
Country	Netherlands
Year	2000
A1	The Beauty Of Silence (Original Mix)
B1	The Beauty Of Silence (Johan Gielen Essential Dark Mix)

SYNCROTRON
—Deep Thought

Label	Frankfurt Beat Productions
Catalogue	901022.6
Country	Germany
Year	1994
A1	Deep Thought (Remix)
A2	Space Port
B1	Molecular Analizer
B2	Deep Thought (Basic)

SYNERGY
—Hello Strings

Label	Armind
Catalogue	ARMD1014
Country	Netherlands
Year	2005
A1	Hello Strings (Original Mix)
B1	Hello Strings (Flash Brothers Remix)

SYSTEM F
—Out Of The Blue

Label	Tsunami
Catalogue	TSU6008
Country	Netherlands
Year	1999
A1	Out Of The Blue (Original Mix)
B1	Out Of The Blue (Lucien's Big Trance Mix)
B2	Out Of The Blue (Super Secret)

SYSTEMATIC PARTS
—Deja Vu

Label	King Size Records
Catalogue	KINGSIZE002
Country	Germany
Year	1997
A1	Deja Vu
B1	Confluence

SYZYGY
—Can I Dream?

Label	Rising High Records
Catalogue	RSN78
Country	United Kingdom
Year	1994
A1	Can I Dream?
A2	Liberation
B1	Never Come Down
B2	Albania

S.P.X.
—Straight To The Point

Label	Smash Trax
Catalogue	ST006
Country	Netherlands
Year	2000
A1	Straight To The Point (Original Mix)
B2	Straight To The Point

(Ambassador Mix)

TASTEXPERIENCE
FEATURING NATASHA PEARL
—*Summersault*
Label	Manifesto
Catalogue	TASDJ1/2
Country	United Kingdom
Year	1997
A1	Summersault (Tall Paul Mix)
B1	Summersault (Original Mix)

TAUCHER
—*Waters*
Label	Liquid Records
Catalogue	LQS004-6
Country	Germany
Year	1996
A1	Waters (Phase III)
B1	Waters (Phase IV)

TECHNIQUE
—*Sun Is Shining*
Label	Creation Records
Catalogue	CRE306T
Country	United Kingdom
Year	1999
A1	Sun Is Shining (Brothers In Rhythm Club Mix)
B1	Sun Is Shining (Mash Up Matt Remix)

TEKARA
—*Breathe In You*
Label	3 Beat Records
Catalogue	3BTT36
Country	United Kingdom
Year	1997
A1	Breathe In You (Tekara Original Mix)
B1	Breathe In You (Lost Tribe Remix)

THE AMBUSH
—*Everlast*
Label	Grand Casino Records
Catalogue	GC002-6
Country	Germany
Year	1999
A1	Everlast
B1	Everlast (Dub Mix)

THE ARC
—*Skinjobs EP*
Label	Inter 1 Records
Catalogue	INT0001
Country	United Kingdom
Year	1994
A1	Skinjobs
A2	Betty's Desire
B1	Something Wonderful
B2	Dreamaway Greenaway

THE AURANAUT
—*People Want To Be Needed*
Label	Barracuda
Catalogue	DIVE003
Country	United Kingdom
Year	1999
A1	People Want To Be Needed (Original Mix)
B1	People Want To Be Needed (The Tea Freaks 'Special Brew' Remix)
B2	People Want To Be Needed (Planet Heaven Remix)

THE FUTURE SOUND OF LONDON
—*Papua New Guinea*
Label	Jumpin' & Pumpin'
Catalogue	12TOT17
Country	United Kingdom
Year	1991
A1	Papua New Guinea (Dali Mix)
B1	Papua New Guinea (Dumb Child Of Q)
B2	Papua New Guinea (Qube Mix)

THE GREEN MARTIAN
—*End Of The Earth*
Label	Tranceportation
Catalogue	TP98013
Country	Belgium
Year	1998
A1	End Of The Earth (Instrumental Cut)
A2	End Of The Earth (Director's Vocal Cut)
B1	Out From The Deep
B2	Reformation

THE INFERNAL MACHINE
—*Realistic*
Label	Sadie Records
Catalogue	SADIE004
Country	Netherlands
Year	2000
A1	Realistic (Original Mix)
B1	Realistic (Stef Remix)

THE MARTIAN
—*Cosmic Movement/Star Dancer*
Label	Red Planet
Catalogue	RP2
Country	United States
Year	1993
A1	Cosmic Movement
B1	Star Dancer

THE MYSTERY
—*Mystery*
Label	RR Records
Catalogue	RR000
Country	Netherlands
Year	2001
A1	The Mystery (Original Mix)
B1	The Mystery (Guitar Mix)

THE QUEST
—*C Sharp*
Label	Redemption
Catalogue	REDEM001
Country	United Kingdom

Year 1999
A1 C Sharp (Original Mix)
B1 C Sharp (Bhaskar Dandona Remix)

THE SOURCE EXPERIENCE
−*The Source Experience*
Label R&S Records
Catalogue RS93027
Country Belgium
Year 1993
A1 The Source Experience
B1 Kamikaze
B2 Release The Pressure
C1 Mental Rider
D1 Elektra

THE TALISMAN & HUDSON
−*Leaving Planet Earth*
Label C.S.M.F. Records
Catalogue CSMF13
Country United Kingdom
Year 1997
A1 Leaving Planet Earth
B1 Distant Shores

THE THRILLSEEKERS
−*Synaesthesia*
Label Neo
Catalogue NEO12016
Country United Kingdom
Year 1999
A1 Synaesthesia (Ylem Remix Mix)
B1 Synaesthesia (En Motion Mix)

THE TRAVELLER & IN MOTION
−*Believe*
Label Vicious Vinyl
Catalogue VV12036
Country Australia
Year 1998
A1 Believe (Original Mix)
B1 Believe (Key South Remix)

THE VISIONS OF SHIVA
−*Perfect Day*
Label MFS
Catalogue MFS7022-0
Country Germany
Year 1992
A1 Perfect Day
B1 Perfect Night
B2 Perfect Morning

THE VOLUNTEERS
−*Sun Down*
Label Eye Q Records
Catalogue EYEQ007
Country Germany
Year 1992
A1 Sun Down
B1 Summer Frequency

THIRD MAN
−*Planet Hunters/Solar Cycle*
Label Hook Recordings
Catalogue HK015
Country UK
Year 1996
A1 Planet Hunters (Arrangement One)
A2 Planet Hunters (Arrangement Two)
B1 Solar Cycle (Arrangement One)
B2 Solar Cycle (Arrangement Two)

THOMAS DATT
−*2v2*
Label Discover
Catalogue DISCOVER10
Country United Kingdom
Year 2004
A1 2V2 (Original Mix)
B1 2v2 (John Askew Remix)

THREE DRIVES ON A VINYL
−*Greece 2000*
Label Massive Drive Recordings
Catalogue MD003
Country Netherlands
Year 1997
A1 Greece 2000
B1 Not Overdrive
B2 Piano Freq.

THREE 'N ONE
−*Reflect*
Label Fire Recordings
Catalogue FIRE135
Country Germany
Year 1996
A1 Reflect
B1 Down In The Hole

TILLMANN UHRMACHER
−*On The Run*
Label Fog Area Trance
Catalogue FOGTRANCE154
Country Germany
Year 2001
A1 On The Run (Ocean To Shore Club Extended)
B1 On The Run (Pole To Pole Experimental)

TILT
−*Invisible*
Label Hooj Choons
Catalogue HOOJ73F
Country United Kingdom
Year 1999
A1 Invisible (Lost Tribe Vocal Mix)
B1 What's This? (Tilt's Tunnel Mix)

TOMCRAFT
−*Loneliness*
Label Kosmo Records
Catalogue KOS2042
Country Germany
Year 2002
A1 Loneliness (Klub Mix)
B1 Loneliness (Muc Mix)

TOTAL ECLIPSE
−*Waiting For A New Life*
Label TIP Records
Catalogue TIP002

Country United Kingdom
Year 1994
A1 Waiting For A New Life
B1 Transparent Mind
B2 Born Bole

TRANCELINER
—The Dream
Label Tesseract Records
Catalogue TES015-5
Country Netherlands
Year 1994
A1 The Dream
B1 The Heat
B2 The Dream (Dream Mix)

TRANCEPARENTS
—Child I II III
Label Heidi Of Switzerland
Catalogue HOS009
Country United Kingdom
Year 1993
A1 Child One
A2 Child Two
B1 Child Three
B2 The Unborn

TRANCEPORTER
—Open Up Your Mind
Label Spacemate Recordings
Catalogue SM1210
Country Germany
Year 1992
A1 Open Up Your Mind
B1 Base
B2 Trancexual

TRANQUIL VOICE
—Acid India
Label Circuit Records
Catalogue LAP2
Country United Kingdom
Year 1993
A1 Acid India (Little Rascal Remix)
B1 Acid India (Original Mix)
B2 Numunah

TRANSA
—Supernova/Transtar
Label UG
Catalogue UG021
Country United Kingdom
Year 1999
A1 Supernova
B1 Transtar

TRANSFORM
—Transformation
Label Cyclotron
Catalogue LEPTONE17
Country Germany
Year 1991
A1 Transformation (Media Mix)
A2 Transformation (Club Mix)
B1 Trans Out (Chill Mix #3)
B2 Trans Out (Chill Mix #3)

TRANSFORMER 2
—Pacific Symphony
Label Round And Round
Catalogue RR9202
Country Belgium
Year 1992
A1 Pacific Symphony
B1 Whistle Tune

TROPE
—Amphetamine
Label Prolekult
Catalogue KULT009
Country United Kingdom
Year 1995
A1 Amphetamine (Original Mix)
B1 Amphetamine (Baby Doc Mix)
C1 Amphetamine (DJ Misjah + Groovehead Mix)
D1 Amphetamine (Red Jerry Mix)

T.L.T.
—Kubik
Label Xtra Nova
Catalogue XN4716
Country Belgium
Year 1997
A1 Kubik (Trance Mix)
A2 Kubik (Special Mix)
B1 Kubik (Original Mix)
B2 Kubik (Seventh Side Mix)

U

ULYSSES
—Prisma EP
Label Noom Records
Catalogue NOOM002-12
Country Germany
Year 1993
A1 Dream 'N' Trance
A2 Whales 2 Females
B1 R U Ready
B2 K.J's Flight

UNION JACK
—Two Full Moons And A Trout/Lollypop Man
Label Platipus
Catalogue PLAT06
Country United Kingdom
Year 1993
A1 Two Full Moons And A Trout
B1 Lollypop Man

UNREAL
—Phenomenon
Label Formaldehyd
Catalogue FORM013
Country Germany
Year 1994
A1 Phenomenon
B1 After Hours

UTAH SAINTS
—Lost Vagueness
Label Echo
Catalogue ECDJ1051

Country	United Kingdom
Year	2000
A1	Lost Vagueness (Oliver Lieb's Main Mix)
B1	Lost Vagueness (Josh Wink's Deep Dub)
C1	Lost Vagueness (Josh Wink's Deep Interpretation)
D1	Lost Vagueness (Oliver Lieb's Dub Mix)

UTASIA
−Stratosphere

Label	NOW! Records
Catalogue	NOW!09
Country	Germany
Year	1993
A1	Stratosphere
A2	Stratosphere (Let's Have A Break Mix)
B1	Stratosphere (No Beat Mix)
B2	Unknown Track

V

VANA IMAGO
−Tesi

Label	Trance Communications Records
Catalogue	TRC2005
Country	Italy
Year	1995
A1	Tesi
B1	Antitesi
B2	Sintesi

VAPOURSPACE
−Gravitational Arch Of 10

Label	Plus 8 Records
Catalogue	PLUS8023
Country	Canada
Year	1993
A1	Gravitational Arch Of 10
B1	Paradox Of Time Dilation
B2	The Cold Air

VEIT
−Sky

Label	Black Hole Recordings
Catalogue	BH149-5
Country	Netherlands
Year	2002
A1	Sky (Magik Muzik Remix)
B1	Sky (Hardy Heller's Down To Earth Mix)
B2	Sky (Original Mix)

VELOCITY
−Lust

Label	Superstition
Catalogue	SUPERSTITION2009
Country	Germany
Year	1993
A1	Lust
B1	Future
B2	Room

VELVET GIRL
−Velvet

Label	Green Martian
Catalogue	GM-2001-035
Country	Belgium
Year	2001
A1	Velvet (Vocal Club Mix)
A2	Velvet (Vocal Trance Mix)
B1	Velvet (Chiller Twist Cosmosis Remix)

VERACOCHA
−Carte Blanche

Label	Deal Records
Catalogue	DEAL022
Country	Netherlands
Year	1999
A1	Carte Blanche
B1	Drafting

VERNON
−Wonderer

Label	Eye Q Records
Catalogue	4509-92035-0
Country	Germany
Year	1993
A1	Wonderer (Vocal Mix)
B1	Wonderer (Instrumental Mix)
B2	Wonderer (Acid Mix)

VIMANA
−We Came/Dreamtime

Label	Black Hole Recordings
Catalogue	BH108-5
Country	Netherlands
Year	1999
A1	We Came
B1	Dreamtime

VINCENT DE MOOR
−Fly Away

Label	VC Recordings
Catalogue	VCRT87
Country	United Kingdom
Year	2001
A1	Fly Away (Yves Deruyter Progress Mix)
A2	Fly Away (Original Mix)
B1	Fly Away (Thrillseekers Remix)

VIRTUAL SYMMETRY
−Discovered Theme

Label	Eye Q Records
Catalogue	EYEQ010
Country	Germany
Year	1993
A1	Discovered Theme
B1	See You
B2	Virtual House

VIRUS
−Sun

Label	Perfecto
Catalogue	PERF107T
Country	United Kingdom
Year	1995
A1	Sun (Jam El Mar Mix)

B1	Sun (Man With No Name Mix)
B2	Sun (Oakenfold/Osborne Mix)

VOYAGE
—Beyond Time/OAF
Label	I.T.P. Recordings
Catalogue	ITP004
Country	United Kingdom
Year	1994
A1	Beyond Time...
B1	OAF (Chordless)
B2	OAF (Chord)

W

WAY OUT WEST FEATURING MISS JOANNA LAW
—The Gift
Label	Deconstruction
Catalogue	74321401911
Country	United Kingdom
Year	1996
A1	The Gift (Original Mix)
B1	The Gift (Club Mix)

WEEKEND WORLD
—The Word/Outsider
Label	Yoshitoshi Recordings
Catalogue	YR064
Country	United States
Year	2001
A1	The Word (Dub)
B1	Outsider (Dub)
C1	Outsider
D1	The Word

WHIRLPOOL
—Under The Sun
Label	Deepblue Records
Catalogue	TRR004
Country	United Kingdom
Year	2004
A1	Under The Sun (Solarstone Remix)
B1	Under The Sun (Filo And Peri Lighthouse Mix)
B2	Under The Sun (Markus Schulz Remix)

WHITEROOM
—The Whiteroom
Label	Liquid Asset
Catalogue	ASSET12017
Country	United Kingdom
Year	2004
A1	The Whiteroom (Original Mix)
B1	The Whiteroom (BJammin Remix)

WILLIAM ORBIT
—Barber's Adagio For Strings
Label	Warner Elektra Atlantic
Catalogue	WEA247T
Country	United Kingdom
Year	1999
A1	Barber's Adagio For Strings (Ferry Corsten Remix)
B1	Barber's Adagio For Strings (Original Mix)

WIPPENBERG
—Neurodancer
Label	Hyper Hype
Catalogue	HH0176
Country	Germany
Year	1995
A1	Neurodancer (Original Mix)
B1	Neurodancer (Neuronoid Mix)
B2	Neurodancer (Club Mix)

WIRE WALKER
—Body-X-Periment/La Troisieme Dimension
Label	Cool Summer Cuts
Catalogue	CSC002
Country	Germany
Year	1993
A1	Body-X-Periment
B1	La Troisieme Dimension

W.P. ALEX REMARK
—Piramid
Label	Dream Records
Catalogue	DREAM010
Country	Italy
Year	1995
A1	Piramid (In Dream)
B1	Piramid (Acquatic Version)
B2	Piramid (Experimental Mix)

X

XME
—Automatic Lover
Label	Tunnel Records
Catalogue	TR004
Country	Germany
Year	1993
A1	Automatic Overdrive
B1	Automatic Lover
B2	Automatic X

X-CABS
—Neuro/Outcast
Label	Bellboy Records
Catalogue	BL007
Country	United Kingdom
Year	1995
A1	Neuro
B1	Outcast

X-DREAM FEATURING PLANET B.E.N.
—The 5th Dimension
Label	Tunnel Records
Catalogue	TR006
Country	Germany
Year	1993
A1	The 5th Dimension
B1	The 5th Dimension (Rush Mix)
B2	The 5th Dimension (Cosmix)

X-FORM
—X-Form
Label	Vertikal Records
Catalogue	VRT001
Country	Italy
Year	1995
A1	Pleasure Voyage (Lunar Mix)

B1	Pleasure Voyage (Apollo Mix)
C1	O-Zone (Space Dub)
D1	Oise (Hardware Mix)

X-TRACKS
—Plan '94
Label	Off Sound Records
Catalogue	OFS001
Country	Italy
Year	1994
A1	Plan '94 (Chapter 1)
A2	Plan '94 (Ethereal Mix)
B1	Plan '94 (The Voyage)

Y

Y TRAXX
—Mystery Land
Label	Xtra Nova
Catalogue	XN4770
Country	Belgium
Year	1998
A1	Mystery Land (Sickboys Courtyard Mix)
B1	Mystery Land (Original Mix)

YAHEL & EYAL BARKAN
—Voyage
Label	In Trance We Trust
Catalogue	ITWT320-5
Country	Netherlands
Year	2000
A1	Voyage
B1	Liquid Paradise
B2	I Believe

YAKARI
—Tranquiliser EP
Label	Loop Records
Catalogue	LOOP001
Country	Sweden
Year	1994
A1	Positive Transphere
A2	Lotus Trance
B1	The Sound Ordeal
B2	Water Of Tranquility

YANTRA
—360
Label	Synewave London
Catalogue	SWUK02
Country	United Kingdom
Year	1994
A1	360
B1	The Birth Of Stars

YILMAZ ALTANHAN
—Eighties
Label	Anjunabeats
Catalogue	ANJ-043
Country	United Kingdom
Year	2005
A1	Eighties (Original Mix)
B1	Eighties (Özgür Can Remix)

YOJI BIOMEHANIKA
—A Theme From Banginglobe
Label	Hellhouse Recordings
Catalogue	HELL08
Country	United Kingdom
Year	2002
A1	A Theme From Banginglobe (Original Mix)
B1	A Theme From Banginglobe (System F Remix)

YOKOTA
—Panicwaves
Label	Harthouse
Catalogue	HH044
Country	Germany
Year	1994
A1	Panicwaves
B1	A Sonic Fairy Tale

YOMANDA
—Synth & Strings
Label	Manifesto
Catalogue	FESX59
Country	United Kingdom
Year	1999
A1	Synth & Strings (Original Mix)
B1	Egg 'n' Cress
B2	Synth & Strings (Joe Fandango's Mitsubishi Mix)

YORK
—The Awakening
Label	Suck Me Plasma
Catalogue	SUCK130-12
Country	Germany
Year	1999
A1	OTB (On The Beach)
B1	The Reachers Of Civilisation

YVES DERUYTER
—Music-Non-Stop
Label	Bonzai Records
Catalogue	BR-2002-173
Country	Belgium
Year	2002
A1	Music-Non-Stop (Original Mix)
B1	Music-Non-Stop (Hard Wave Edit)
B2	Back To Earth (DJ Scot Project Remix)

Z

ZEN PARADOX
—The Light At The End…?
Label	Psy-Harmonics
Catalogue	PSY-006
Country	Australia
Year	1993
A1	The Light At The End…?
B1	Say Goodbye To The Dark Place
B2	Minon

ZERO GRAVITY
—Sensorium EP
Label	Rhinebeat
Catalogue	RB1211
Country	Germany
Year	1992

A1	Sensorium
B1	Just Cry
B2	Light The Incense

ZYON
—No Fate

Label	Eye Q Records
Catalogue	9031-77032-0
Country	Germany
Year	1992
A1	No Fate (No Fate Mix)
B1	No Fate (Radio Mix)
B2	No Fate (Struggle Continous Mix)

#

4 VOICE
—Eternal Spirit

Label	Rising High Records
Catalogue	RSN67
Country	United Kingdom
Year	1993
A1	Eternal Spirit (Northern Mix)
A2	Fairlight 1
B1	Eternal Spirit (Southern Mix)
B2	Light

8 WONDERS
—The Morning After

Label	Somatic Sense
Catalogue	SOMATIC004
Country	Netherlands
Year	2004
A1	The Morning After (Original)
B1	The Morning After (Octagen's Night Before Mix)

AIRWAVE—*Alone In The Dark* (2000)
Laurent Véronnez, Belgium

A man with many hats, Belgian artist Laurent Véronnez has composed hundreds of tracks for no less than thirty-five projects, including the monikers Airwave, Cloud 69, L-Vee, Lolo, Planisphere, The Green Martian, V-One and Velvet Girl. Véronnez has been closely associated with Bonzai Records since 1996. Clocking in at almost eleven minutes, Alone In The Dark turned out to be one of his deepest musical adventures.

"I discovered electronic music via Vangelis around the age of nine and my interest further developed through acts such as Tangerine Dream, Jean-Michel Jarre, OMD and Depeche Mode. This was around 1987, when house music was just born and the new beat 'micro-culture' was about to explode in Belgium. In 1992, at the age of fourteen and after a critical moment in my personal life, I met a few guys who would become very close friends and decided to take the plunge into playing keyboards. At that point, I had no interest in creating electronic music. The genre was just something I listened to on the side.

Yet these electronic sounds kept attracting me: I just couldn't find my own identity in this club music until I heard Blue Alphabet's Cybertrance (an early Bonzai release) on an obscure radio station in 1994. The same set featured Energy 52's Café Del Mar in its original version as well as many other tracks from

German labels such as Eye-Q and MFS—the two avant-garde trance labels from freshly reunited Germany. This sound became my connection to the outside world."

After having recorded about thirty demos, Véronnez finally felt confident enough to release his music but had no idea how to make it in the music business. "As I initially created relaxing ambient electronic music, I remember sending it candidly to Universal Music Group—holding its offices just down my street, but this clearly didn't lead to anything. I don't think my tracks were really good either.

In 1996 I made a shortlist of interesting labels. My list started with Bonzai Records, being the largest dance music label in Belgium at that time. The initial reactions from the Bonzai team were overwhelming. And I was only eighteen years old when we started working together. I never paid a visit to any other label."

After the first successes with small-scale vinyl projects such as PLG, North Pole, Montera and Magnetix, Véronnez eventually broke through to wider recognition with the first release of Fire & Ice—his collaborative studio project with DJ Fire. Véronnez decided to move to Antwerp to focus further on his production work as part of the Bonzai crew.

"That visceral way of making music made Bonzai stand out from other productions at the time. Tracks weren't mixed down properly, the results weren't perfect and, interestingly, nobody cared. It was very underground, unforced and spontaneous. I also used various monikers, as it seemed more convenient to fragment my musical identity into smaller units to avoid confusion amongst listeners. Our idea was to keep people happy with just one for each mind. This was a bit obscure, as most artists didn't have any identity at all except the one on the record."

A string of releases followed and Véronnez' music came to the ears of the generation of Dutch trance DJs around the turn of the century, which would prove crucial in the evolution of his career. Alone In The Dark under his Airwave moniker became particularly relevant.

"The title was based on the fact that I finished this track in the middle of the night, putting myself completely in the dark to listen to the final result. I had the beats, bassline and strings line all sorted, but then my computer crashed. When I re-opened the project, the strings were gone so I started playing something in line with what I played earlier that day. For the first time in my life, I was able to let my heart speak instead of my head and I remember spending hours listening to what I had done in a couple of minutes. These evolving pads were written as you would write for a string ensemble, but I realised that only years later."

Being an avid fan of graphics himself, Véronnez elaborates on the link between sound and imagery. "The purest form of European trance music was born in the minds of German teenagers who desperately wanted to make movie scores. Take that Jam & Spoon remix of The Age Of Love, for example: an image of joy just sparks into your head when that choir sound or breakdown hits you! Those theatrical moments are timeless: they made trance music and still do."

BANCO DE GAIA—*Last Train To Lhasa* (1995)
Toby Marks, United Kingdom

Banco De Gaia is an electronic music project from England, formed by Toby Marks in 1989. Under this alias, Marks crossed various genres and often came to fuse ambient and dub with Arabic and Middle Eastern samples against a bass-heavy reggae, rock or trance rhythm to produce deeply textured tracks that progress layer upon layer—as featured on the single and same-titled album Last Train To Lhasa.

"As a teenager, I was mostly into heavy rock and psychedelia as well as punk when that happened. My biggest influences were probably Pink Floyd, Jimi Hendrix and Frank Zappa. Later on, I became interested in jazz, especially world-fusion stuff by the likes of John MacLaughlin and Miles Davis.

There was a piano in the house when I was growing up and although I didn't know what I was doing I liked to play around on it sometimes. When I was nine years old, I started to play the trumpet and had a fantastic teacher who helped me discover the immense joy in making music. From that point on it was the most important thing in my life.

My interest began to lean towards electronic music in 1987, when I heard Paid In Full (Coldcut Remix) by Eric B and Rakim aired on John Peel's radio show. I had been aware of—and intrigued by—the acid house scene for a couple of years but didn't really get it until I tried to create my own works in 1988. Whether it was trance, house, techno or whatever I was doing, I wasn't bothered about sticking rigidly to genres."

The singularity of Marks' work lay in the fact he was using and emulating sounds from other countries and cultures—often mistakenly classified by some as 'world music'. "Back then, I was very interested in building rhythms out of unusual and natural sounds: I had already done a helicopter and a steam train seemed a very obvious thing to do. I was surprised to hear that no one else seemed to have done it already. I added various other bits and pieces that I had lying around to it, as there wasn't a clear plan—just trying things to see what sounded good together. I think it was a response to our rapidly expanding awareness of the rest of the world through modern media and more affordable travel.

During my time in the Middle East, I came to recognise that all music is built on fundamentally similar principles and, whilst it might sound alien and strange at first, the familiar patterns and relationships soon start to come through and we respond as well to that as to our own indigenous music. Interestingly, it was a sample of Israeli singer Ofra Haza on an Eric B. and Rakim track that first caught my attention and made me think: 'I want to do that'."

Last Train To Lhasa was given its title by Marks' wife, his girlfriend at the time. "It was the last track I wrote for the album and I was trying to think of a title when she came up with that. It starts with a train sample so it seemed a reasonable choice. Once we had the title, I decided to use that as the title of the album too. And as I was interested in—and saddened by—the situation in Tibet at the time, I decided to use the album to try to raise awareness about the plight of the Tibetan people at the hands of their Chinese occupiers.

These days, the track has become a bit of a joke in our house that if people know who Banco De Gaia is, it's usually because of 'the one with the train on'. Certainly the marketing push behind Last Train To Lhasa meant that it reached a much wider audience than any of my other tracks and albums. Yet I don't think it's significantly better than a lot of other tracks."

For Marks, acid house, house, techno and early spin-offs were very much a product of that time. "Later evolutions into trance in its various forms feel like just that, evolutions, all of which grew from what came before and no doubt will continue to. It seems like there are some pretty rigid rules in some areas of the scene now with not so much innovation going on but I guess that is inevitable."

In all logic, Marks never considered himself as part of any other genre or subculture. "I always saw the post-acid house dance scene that I was involved with as a continuation of the sixties spirit of Woodstock. It had that same sense of exploration, both inner and outer and a sense of breaking down barriers and of strangers being friends. I guess at heart it was all about unity, coming together as one and the music was a great vehicle for that, as it has been for thousands of years."

BARBARELLA—*My Name Is Barbarella* (1992)
Ralf Hildenbeutel, Germany

Ralf Hildenbeutel played an important role in placing the Frankfurt-based record labels Eye Q and Harthouse on the map, which have both proven to be key platforms for the rise and development of trance music in the early nineties. His solo productions were brought to light under various monikers including Icon, Mignon and Progressive Attack. Yet, his most notorious recordings were achieved as part of collaborative projects, including Barbarella and The Essence Of Nature (both together with Sven Väth), Cygnus X (alongside Matthias Hoffman), Earth Nation (with Marcus Deml) and Odyssee Of Noises (in collaboration with Matthias Hoffman and Steffen Britzke).

"My classical music education started when I was nine years old, playing the piano. It didn't take me long to recognise that music would play a big part in my life. As time went by, I started playing in bands before getting my first keyboard. In the eighties I got more interested in electronic music, being influenced by artists such as Jean-Michel Jarre, Kraftwerk, Ultravox and other typical synth-rock bands from the era.

At the time I was creating my first home recordings with the tape-to-tape technique, layering multiple synthesizers. This fascination for instrumental electronic music grew on me over time, even though my classical background remained dear to my heart."

Hildenbeutel then found himself projected in the heart of the then-nascent trance movement. Interestingly and although he has always considered himself a solo producer, many of his early productions were collaborative projects.

"Working together with someone else is a completely different experience: it's always interesting and fascinating. The Barbarella project was my first collaboration with Sven Väth. I met him just shortly before through Matthias Hoffman (aka A.C. Boutsen) and Steffen Britzke (aka B-Zet), whom I knew from playing together in a band years before. They worked with Sven on his Organisation For Fun album back in 1988.

Sven and I started this 12" project with the concept of a trancy A-side and a harder B-side. My Name Is Barbarella was born and this was basically our first common release. It did really well in the clubs and we continued to do some more 12" releases with the same concept."

Eventually, the duo wrote enough material to complete their debut long-player, titled The Art Of Dance. Barbarella was Hildenbeutel's first collaborative piece with Väth and is considered the starting point of a long-term collaboration between both artists.

"Back then, it wasn't very common for DJs to work with musicians on club-oriented material. This unique combination made our sound even more special. The musician brings in elements that a DJ doesn't know, while a DJ brings in elements that a musician isn't aware of.

Musicians such as Steffen Britzke, Matthias Hoffmann and myself have this strong musical background. When mixed with the outstanding feel for arrangements and sounds of a DJ such as Sven Väth, it results in this fresh and inspirational output. I think you could hear that in our music."

Hildenbeutel still has vivid memories of that era. "The early nineties happened to be very intense and full of fantastic moments, starting from the excitement of producing music in the studio without any boundaries to hearing Sven play it from DAT tapes in clubs during the weekend and by playing with my act Earth Nation at these large, outstanding events such as the Montreux Jazz Festival.

Trance was new and fresh and this mixture of hard beats, monotony and melodic elements reflected the zeitgeist very well. It's hard to compare with today, as electronic music has been around for years by now. However, all those different subgenres out there still make electronic music exciting."

Hildenbeutel's personal career also moved ahead over the years. "The digital revolution around the turn of the millennium had a major impact on the music industry. Everybody had to learn how to cope with this radical change of not making money with music sales. I was lucky enough to be able to concentrate on film music, which gave me the opportunity to earn money without depending on music sales. But at the end of the day, I believe things are rather similar in the music industry: there will always be both major players and independent actors."

COAST 2 COAST FEATURING DISCOVERY
—*Home* (2000)
Phil Johnston, Ireland

The discography of Irish duo Coast 2 Coast, alias Gleave Dobbin and Phil Johnston, spans a rather limited output with just four singles. Yet, their debut record titled Home became an instant hit around the turn of the millennium. The track, characterised by its powerful yet mellifluous vocals, made its way into the record bags of trance-friendly DJs the world over.

"I have been making music since I was about eleven or twelve years old. My Dad got me an Atari ST home computer for Christmas, yet I hadn't realised it was possible to now make music. Back then, I liked playing the guitar, keyboards and made up songs and recorded them on a Sharp X-bass ghetto blaster. When I figured out what the Atari ST could do and learned about midi, I ended up selling the ST to fund our band in a recording session.

Instead, I got my hands on a PC, bought an EMU sound card which could do sixteen parts—that was when I really got into Cubase. When I turned seventeen years old, I got my first 'proper' synthesizer, a Yamaha SY85. A new world unfolded, as it had a sampler and I was able to load my own drums—which were mostly ripped from Chemical Brothers or Hardfloor tracks."

Not long after, Johnston was working in a music store

selling synths and pro audio gear. "I think I was about nineteen or twenty years old. I also had a small studio around the corner, in the back room of a club called the Network. The venue had loads of progressive DJs playing, such as Anthony Pappa, John Digweed, Ian Osia and Nick Warren, which got me more into trance.

The deal was that I got the room for free if I gave the resident DJs—JayKay & Mark Jackson—studio time. I hooked up with Paul Hamill aka Psycatron, who at the time was doing a journalism course. Paul helped me with marketing and we did a few tracks together, including Sliver, which got some plays by Paul van Dyk and Nick Warren.

> "We just loved BT and Paul van Dyk and wanted to get somewhere close to that level of production."

"This track got noticed by Billy Dunseath, who was running RGB at the time and soon turned into Religion Music. So Paul Hamill set up a meeting and RGB offered me a job in their studio to basically work on remixes and production work.

Gleave Dobbin, who was part of Billy Dunseath's DJ roster, had an idea for a track. He wanted to do a remake of a house track called Freaky Dreamer by the artist of the same name that came out back in

1990. So we kinda got halfway into it and decided to write our own vocals instead of doing the remake, so I called up my sister's best mate Penny. She came down, stayed for a few days and came up with the vocal hook.

That's how Coast 2 Coast was formed. We knew we had something special here, so we wanted to make sure it sounded great. So I probably spent about two months and twelve hours a day, trying to get the riffs and sounds right on it. If I'm honest I'd say it was mainly the vocals of Home that really seemed to draw people in. After this, we happened to be DJing a fair bit and got some good gigs, such as playing Privilege in Ibiza—although I was pretty terrible at it. I preferred being in the studio."

Johnston's best memories were the times they would go out with Chris and Robbie from Agnelli & Nelson and get them to play their new tracks, to hear how it sounded in the club. Next, Johnston and Dobbin would head back to the studio and do some tweaks.

"Being different wasn't that important to us, as we were really young and didn't really know what we were doing. We just loved BT and Paul van Dyk and wanted to get somewhere close to that level of production.

After that, things got a bit tricky. RGB was unhappy that we wanted our own studio: at the time we were paying them a shitload to rent their place so when we moved into our own place they basically stopped giving us any of our royalties and were holding back compilation income. It was a bit of a nightmare...

"We survived doing remixes and some ghost producing, but the whole thing put me off the music industry. I found it really hard to write stuff after that and ended up doing some teaching instead. So it's mixed emotions really. I'm very proud of the track, but it was also a missed opportunity. As said, we ultimately got tricked into giving up the copyrights of the track for our freedom from RGB. It was a total scam looking back.

We weren't the only artists to get totally shafted. It was a really painful period. So all the new remixes and new labels have nothing to do with us. We had no say and didn't get a penny. I felt like all the shit with RGB was a distraction from just making tunes and gigging. Although maybe it's fate, as I love what I do now and maybe I wouldn't have been doing it if things had gone better with the music."

COSMIC BABY—*Fantasia* (1994)
Harald Blüchel, Germany

Harald Blüchel is considered one of the founding fathers of the trance movement in Germany during the early nineties. Most of his visionary works can be tied to his Cosmic Baby moniker, along with some choice collaborations including Energy 52 (together with Paul Schmitz-Moormann), Futurhythm (alongside Christian Graupner and Jürgen Stöckemann) and The Visions Of Shiva (with Paul van Dyk). Blüchel's release Fantasia, an emotionally charged crossover of symphonic elements and lushly textured electronics, became a benchmark for trance music in the early days.

"Ever since I started making music as a child, I was particularly attracted to atmospheric sounds, strong melodies and repetitive structures. I discovered the piano at the age of four and making music became my way of interpreting my thoughts about life. Playing and composing music became my most profound opportunity to build up an identity.

Around the age of twelve, I stumbled upon new German music like Cluster, Kraftwerk and Tangerine Dream and this discovery struck me like a thunderbolt. I had never heard such music and yet it felt as if it had always been in me."

Blüchel's next inspirations came from artists like Brian Eno, Wim Mertens and Giorgio Moroder, as well as

Donna Summer's I Feel Love. These major influences, together with his classical background, strengthened Blüchel's excitement for synthesizers, as well as his attitude towards creating a signature sound.

"I wanted to create music as a transformed synthesis of mental and physical energy, music for body and spirit at the same time, based on electronic instruments. As synthesizers were incredibly expensive at the end of the seventies, I had to forge my own handmade electronic sounds out of alternative sources. I used my (prepared) piano, sounds from the radio, lots of percussion and two tape recorders for ping-pong recording.

Later on, I would add a Fender Rhodes E-piano, my first semi-electronic instrument and a Roland TR-606 drum machine, before the digital synthesizer was introduced during the mid-eighties. I was finally able to get my hands on all these beloved instruments and it all really felt like entering paradise."

When Blüchel started studying composition at the Hochschule der Künste in West Berlin in 1986, he came in touch with this very small group of people who were involved in the—than almost unknown—acid, house and techno scene. "And those were the same 150 people who would make the first Love Parade happen in 1989! I met new friends, became part of a family and belonged to a movement."

Blüchel's debut album, Stellar Supreme, helped define his status on the international map of techno-trance music. With his follow-up album, Thinking About Myself, Blüchel aimed at expanding this sound spectrum entirely.

"Most of the pieces on the album were already composed when I returned to the studio for two months. The abstract topic of Fantasia had been brewing in my mind for a long time already. I made at least twenty fragments which circled around this idea. They all sounded different and targeted just partial aspects of what I wanted to express. So all of them were thrown away, but they had all reverberated at a subconscious level and were, therefore, part of a necessary process. Eventually, the Fantasia we know was created in just one night—out of the blue, so to say.

Hence, what we call 'random' is much more connected to inner preparation and resonating conditions than most of us may realise. Being creative has, in my experience, less to do with mood and moment. It is rather an evolutionary process, it has to do with patience and readiness and also the perseverance of bringing a challenging idea to the world."

In retrospect, the 1993-1995 period stands out in Blüchel's discography as the heyday of his output under the moniker of Cosmic Baby. "Back then, electronic music offered a whole spectrum of styles. Almost every day, a new and interesting musical approach made its way to our ears. Structures and global networks developed constantly, ripening and attaining a professional level without being controlled by the mainstream industry.

Also, techno offered an alternative lifestyle, an option to live beyond common categories. Being an active part of it was a true gift. I was lucky enough to be in the right place at the right time, equipped with my personal headspace, skills and open attitude towards the unexpected. This matched perfectly with something that was yet to find its definition. I was lucky and, retrospectively, very grateful for the opportunity of having become part of this movement, which enabled complete freedom to create whatever we wanted.

"The result of this phenomenon, which took place all over the world and at about the same time, was an explosion of groundbreaking sounds and styles. There was positive mutual feedback and global teamwork. Nothing was pre-programmed and rules weren't defined yet.

All in all, this period up to 1999 brought wonderful musical innovations—and, naturally, tons of mediocre and cheap-sounding mass productions. But the best examples will live forever, as their potential will remain inspirational to future generations."

In 1999, Blüchel withdrew himself from the techno scene. "There was no reason for me to end up like other trance superstars. I am too much of an artist and maverick, rather than a businessman or someone whose ego depends on the quantity of success. I had to let go of Cosmic Baby in order to have time and space for new musical and personal directions. My ambitions and affections tended towards contemporary classical ways of composing, not towards self-satisfied football stadium-sized shows—and that included appropriate musical confection."

DAVID FORBES—*Questions*
(Must Be Asked) (1998)
David Forbes, Scotland

Hailing from Scotland, producer David Forbes took his first steps in the world of alternative music in the nineties via the hardcore scene, though it's with his first formal record Questions (Must Be Asked) that the Scottish artist quite drastically shifted the trance music paradigm.

"When I started listening to trance music, the word hadn't actually been created yet. Many of the early trance artists were hardcore producers that had moved on from a declining scene around the late nineties. I'm sure people like Armin van Buuren and Ferry Corsten also produced some hardcore records. Personally, I was specifically excited about labels such as Noom and R&S, but eventually became heavily influenced by Paul Oakenfold and his Goa-directed Perfecto Fluoro label.

I bought my first gear, an Atari 1040ST home computer and an AKAI S950 sampler, from the money I received for my twenty-first birthday. Back in the days, there were only a few people in Scotland producing dance music, so you had to figure it out yourself.

There was an organisation in the United Kingdom called The Prince's Trust, through which young and aspiring people could apply for funding: I did and ended up getting five thousand Pounds in support.

It wasn't a lot of money in terms of buying studio equipment at the time, yet, I managed to purchase a mixing desk, DAT machine and Roland JV1080 for that sum."

A few years later, following a stream of solid studio productions, Forbes was invited to move into a studio complex owned by Mallorca Lee, a friend who was part of the then-popular Scottish dance act Ultra-Sonic. "Our complex was full of synthesizers and midi cables wiring everywhere and we always shared our equipment. At some point I was able to work with a Waldorf Pulse, which led to the main hook of Questions. The track was finished only four hours later.

Questions became a huge success in the trance scene and it was crazy to see that I started making a lot of money at once. It was quite an experience: the whole process of getting released, signing deals and then watching it snowball into something unstoppable at the time. It was also great seeing my family and girlfriend having that proud grin on their faces, while I was pretty much doing the full press thing on the track, including TV-interviews.

"I was just a young kid who had been successful within the hardcore scene. Yet at some point, the music quality had become really bad, so it was time to pull the rip chord and look out for something else. I wasn't sure if I was even going to continue producing music.

However, because of this record deal and

publishing advances from various labels, I had more money in my bank account than my parents had ever seen. The people in the bank literally thought I was a drug dealer laundering money!"

DELERIUM FEATURING SARAH MCLACHLAN
—*Silence* (1999)
Bill Leeb, Canada

Delerium is a Canadian electronic music duo formed in 1987, originally as a side project of the influential industrial music act, Front Line Assembly. The only constant member throughout its history has been Bill Leeb. The band's musical style has spanned a wide sound spectrum, moving from dark, ethereal ambient to vocal-less industrial soundscapes. Drawing closer to the end of the nineties, the band gained significant popularity via high-profile trance remixes of tracks lifted from their albums Karma and Poem, with Silence being the absolute pinnacle of Delerium's career.

"I moved from Vienna, Austria to Canada at the age of fourteen. Vienna was a very traditional and conservative city and I had never been exposed to any other types of music except choir and classical music before that. I played the violin in school and tried to get my hands on anything I could regarding music and it just struck me.

The first electronic music I heard were works from Kraftwerk and Tangerine Dream, which struck a chord in me. It also evolved from earlier industrial music like Throbbing Gristle and Cabaret Voltaire towards Blue Monday by New Order. When all these releases came out I would go to Odyssey Imports and get everything that I could."

Leeb moved again, to Vancouver, when he was

twenty-one. "The music scene there was new and fresh and I met various interesting people. I met Rhys Fulber at that time and he was only about fourteen years old. We would hang out at record stores and there was a great music scene in Vancouver at the time.

Everything was an inspiration and we just experimented with anything we could regarding music. Once I began producing music myself, I enjoyed experimenting with different sounds—anything from samples and noises we made with different instruments, to vocal samples and basically anything that you could imagine."

> "When DJ Tiësto made his remix of Silence and got a hold of it, it just went with a bang."

Leeb was very closely related to Nettwerk Records in the late nineties and even had an office there when the duo was signed to the label. "Rhys and I had written this instrumental track and it was actually going to be released as an instrumental. Sarah McLachlan was really young, I think only eighteen or nineteen years old and Mark Jowett—the label manager of Nettwerk Records—suggested she should sing on one of our tracks.

We literally sent her the track and she

immediately responded with an idea. Soon after we ended up in Bryan Adams' studio in Vancouver. She jumped over and recorded the lyrics and vocals, which resulted in Silence. We were pretty experimental and used a lot of samples and different sounds, like recordings we made from choirs and monks in churches.

"People had a hard time describing our music, as it came from so many influences and different places. When DJ Tiësto made his remix of Silence and got a hold of it, it just went with a bang. I even heard that he still closes his DJ-sets with Silence sometimes. You'd be surprised how many requests we still get to remix, cover and remake that song."

FICTIVISION VS. C-QUENCE—*Symbols* (2003)
Bart van Wissen, Netherlands

Under the short-lived alias of Fictivision, Dutch artist Bart van Wissen released only four singles over a period of two years. Its most representative claim to fame was under the banner of high-rated label In Trance We Trust—a subdivision of Black Hole Recordings. Released in 2003, Symbols quickly became one of the most unrelentingly euphoric anthems of its time. Aside from the intense breakdown comprising a peak-time-ready main line, the track relies on intricate skeins of revved-up melodies to generate its hair-raising atmosphere.

"You could always hear music in our household. My father played classical music on the piano, my mother sang and played folk and pop songs on the guitar. My parents had quite a diverse record collection, ranging from classical music to pop and rock, including bands like ELO and Dire Straits. Subconsciously, those artists may have had a big influence early on.

My first encounter with electronic music was when a friend gave me a tape copy of Turn Up The Bass—a Dutch compilation series. I had never heard of house music before and it sounded like nothing I had heard before. Later on I discovered more underground material and by the age of twelve years old I was mostly listening to jungle and drum and bass.

"It was the pre-internet age and it was quite hard to find

that kind of music, which made it all the more interesting. In my high school years, I started playing around with a lot of music-production software. I had gotten my first keyboard from my granddad as an eight-year old kid and had learned the basics of playing it.

I had been playing around with MIDI sequencers after my father bought a computer with a sound card on it, but it wasn't until I discovered Impulse Tracker years later that I got serious about music production. I was spending most of my spare time collecting and editing samples and producing tracks."

Working with Reason software made Van Wissen almost accidentally produce trance music, something he hadn't done before. "Before that, I had mostly been working with trackers, meaning my work was sample-based. I had experimented with hardware synthesizers and sequencer software, but hated the complexity of saving projects and restoring them later on.

With Reason, everything I needed was just right there. Ringworld was one of the first tracks I finished. A friend encouraged me to post it on a Dutch online forum called Clubcharts to receive feedback. I got a lot of positive reactions there, which gave me the confidence to send out my first demo.

"The demo ended up in the hands of Peter van Hal, who was the A&R manager for Extrema Records at the time. He wrote back to me that this wasn't really in line with the Extrema material, but he was willing to help me get in touch with the right people, which eventually led to the demo ending up at Black Hole Recordings and Peter being my manager for several years.

In the same year I met Joris van der Straten (C-Quence), who was also active in the Clubcharts community. I had just come up with the melody for what would become Symbols, but was hit with writer's block and couldn't finish it. Joris and I then decided to collaborate on the track: it took us a few hours to finish it."

Symbols became Van Wissen's second and most successful release, which came out on Black Hole's offshoot, In Trance We Trust. "The track got a lot of attention and it really opened doors for me. DJ Tiësto had not only played it as part of his Tiësto in Concert event in 2003, but also included it on the DVD. When I watched the live registration and saw those thousands of people dancing to my music, that was really amazing.

"The Fictivision project ended soon after the release of Symbols, because I felt like I was done with trance music. I was finishing my studies at the time and living off a student loan. Staying up all night to make music was fine for a while. But when I graduated, I needed to get some income, because the music wasn't really bringing in much.

I also felt like the music industry wasn't really for me. Making money with music required a lot of networking and putting yourself in the spotlight, which I hated to do. So I came to terms with the fact that music would be a hobby for me, not a job. So I started working as a software engineer and it just became more difficult to find time to delve into the studio. My last release was around 2009, so I guess I have effectively quit releasing music—but it was never a deliberate decision."

HARMON EYES – *Through The Tunnel* (1995)
Peter Benisch, Sweden

Hailing from Stockholm, Peter Benisch is a classically trained composer who developed a strong interest in synthesizers and computers. Back in the late nineties, Benisch set up Globe Studios in Stockholm alongside fellow producers Adam Beyer, Jesper Dahlbäck and Joel Mull, in parallel to running the company Frost Network, which used to build computers optimised for music production and related operations. His Harmon Eyes project bridged the gap between the deeper sides of both techno and trance, with Through The Tunnel being its flagship track.

"I started listening to music actively when I was about ten years old. At that time, bands like A-ha, Depeche Mode, Erasure and the Pet Shop Boys were popular on the waves and they particularly appealed to me. Back then I had no idea that this music was produced using synthesizers and drum machines.

It felt like an accident that music with electronic sounds made its way into pop music and I happened to fall for it. I started studying classical music, but at the same time realised how much I liked electronic music. These days, artists like Nils Frahm are able to beautifully combine elements from both genres, but back in the days these scenes seemed miles apart.

"In retrospect, making music with the aid of a computer was frowned upon by most traditional musicians. My first serious purchase traces back to when I was sixteen years old. In this pre-internet era, it was extremely difficult to find out what gear to purchase and how to use it. Also, machines were really expensive.

Finally, I decided to buy a sampler: the Ensonic EPS. It seemed like a decent starting point and the music store that sold it had a huge sample library that I could copy for free. The EPS also had a built-in, eight-track sequencer that sounded really nice. If I still had this machine today, I'm sure I would find interesting ways to use it.

This period was considered a mix of trial and error, letting the inspiration flow and just trying to get everything together, in order to create something that would resemble a tune. My driving force was to understand how to use the machines and how others had done so to produce specific sounds. At that time I was also building synthesizers at Nord keyboards, so I was really fascinated by the 'behind the scenes' aspect of music and how sound was created."

The early projects of Benisch were mostly centred around finding where to fit his sounds. "My first releases were made together with Adam Beyer and we basically used to pick a different pseudonym for each label we worked with. I decided to release more ambient sounds under my own name, while Harmon Eyes became my first club-oriented solo project.

The scene was very small back then, so eventually, you just get to know everyone involved in producing electronic music, at least in Stockholm. One of Loop Records' early artists, Cari Lekebusch, got the word around that the label was looking for projects to release, so I sent them a demo. What I really liked about Loop was that they were looking at the bigger picture. The crew set up amazing parties but also released good music. This combination enabled me to play my material live on stage as well."

Benisch' releases spoke to both techno and trance enthusiasts: especially his records as Harmon Eyes, which was put out to pasture after the third single, Through The Tunnel, came out in 1995. "That track was nothing more than me liking the monotonous, trancy techno sound that labels like Music Man put out at the time. I just tried to make something in that direction. I had no idea that the track became an underground gem, but it does make me very happy since that track is also one of my favourite productions.

    The track had little significance for my future career or the development of my productions, however. I was just experimenting with different sounds and styles and trying to advance my capabilities. After finishing a track, it could take up to six to twelve months until the record finally hit the record stores. By the time of the release, I had already moved on. But the feedback I got was really great and that is why I kept making tracks.

"I believe that a lot of releases that had a huge impact on the trance scene were not even intended to be trance tracks when they were first created. More likely, something that fits into a timeline now that you can look back and see how it evolved. I mean, look at Trilithon's Trance Dance 128 album from 1992, for example. It's incredible. It's not difficult to realise the impact it has had when you listen to it today.

Hence, genres have always been confusing to me, though and I have never really felt comfortable using them more than just to give someone a quick idea of what I'm referring to and to be able to have a discussion about various musical topics. For me, it was just natural to like electronic music with strings and melodies, since I had my classically trained background and a combined interest in electronic sounds.

"One can end up being under the impression that artists follow a carefully elaborated plan on how to move on to the next step. Maybe it was like that for others, but I was just trying to make good tracks and hoping that someone would release them so that others might like them as well.

As such, producing music has almost exclusively been a hobby. I was also building synthesizers and have been running a computer company with custom-made models for musicians for thirteen years. Yet, I started a completely new chapter in my life and picked up a study in medicine. Listening to and producing music will never go away though."

JAM & SPOON—*Stella* (1992)
Rolf Ellmer, Germany

Jam & Spoon was a German electronic music duo formed in 1991 in Frankfurt by Rolf Ellmer and Marcus Löffel. Whereas Ellmer (aka Jam El Mar, Trancy Spacer) is a classically trained musician, composer and concert guitarist Löffel (aka Mark Spoon, Spacy Trancer) began his professional career as a cook before shifting directions and working as a DJ and producer in the late eighties. Their single Stella is generally considered to have given birth to the sound of trance music as we know it today.

"I have always been fascinated with music that had specific psychedelic components. My first real, strong influence was Jimmy Hendrix. He wasn't necessarily an electronic musician, but his music was electrifying and had the force and energy of a wild techno record.

I also loved the middle part of Led Zeppelin's Whole Lotta Love as well as Pink Floyd's Dark Side Of The Moon and Wish You Were Here. Later on, Tangerine Dream, Klaus Schulze and Isao Tomita became objects of fascination to me, as well as these horn sounds Keith Emerson created on Emerson, Lake & Palmer's tracks Tarkus and Jerusalem."

From an early age, Ellmer's sole goal has been to make music an important part of his life. Having known Löffel since the late eighties, the duo decided to work together in 1990. "Our first release, under the Dance 2 Trance moniker, followed that year and was released on Suck Me Plasma. The promo release contained two tracks, Dance 2 Trance and We Came In Peace." The artist and track title were amongst the first direct mentions to the term 'trance' to appear on a record centre label.

Subsequently, the duo made an enormous impact in 1992 with their groundbreaking remix of the self-titled single by Age of Love, produced by Bruno Sanchioni and Giuseppe Cherchia from Italy, featuring vocals by Karen Mulder. The original release came out in 1990, the Watch Out For Stella remix was commissioned by React two years later.

"The drop in The Age Of Love was probably the blueprint for all the drops that became so familiar in electronic music. I remember a discussion in the studio with Mark: I was asking him if he was serious about switching off all drums and just let the pads play on. He insisted and it worked perfectly well. It was the genius of Markus that he was brave enough to try unconditional things."

Their first EP as Jam & Spoon, named Tales From A Danceographic Ocean, featured their influential hit Stella. With its dreamy synth line and groove—that was actually taken in bits from Moby's mega-hit Go, released a year earlier, Stella became one of the first tracks to be widely and properly classified as 'trance'.

"That production came out from one of these

lucky moments—just fun and flow in the studio. When we finally had a bunch of tracks assembled, we then aimed to climb the Olympics of all labels at the time—R&S Records. Luckily enough Markus knew Renaat Vandepapeliere, the label owner of R&S, from his DJ-activities and works as an A&R manager at Logic Records. Renaat picked a couple of tracks for our first EP, Tales From A Danceographic Ocean, and the starter pistol was fired."

However, Ellmer still finds it difficult to understand why Stella became a global success. "Some tracks just have that extra gold dust that makes them stand out from the crowd, but it seems impossible to thoroughly explain. It may have been the way we selected our sounds and arranged our tracks, or maybe it just fell right in line with the vibe of the time...

"To me, trance was definitely the sound of the early nineties. It had a lot of that love, peace and hippie thing I experienced back in the late sixties and early seventies. As goes with every genre, some of its original elements may eventually return over time. With its strong community and global appeal, I believe trance will further evolve, without losing its glance."

Markus Löffel died of a heart attack in his Berlin flat, on 11 January 2006 at the age of 39. Ellmer is still active under his Jam El Mar moniker.

Sven Väth at Sensation, 2000 © Pim Warnars

LYRIC & NATALI—*Over Emotion* (2002)
Liran Shoshan, Israel

A driving force of the movement, Israel played an important role in the rise and development of psy-trance music. Though a highly popular genre then, psy-trance wasn't the only product to be pushed from this isolated region, as Liran Shoshan helped the world realise through his cross-pollinated productions. Regardless of his limited discography, Shoshan's works have been acclaimed as some of the genre's finest and found their way into the record bags of many high-profile artists, of which Over Emotion is a perfect example.

"I've always loved playing the organ and took piano lessons from the age of ten, but found my way mostly by developing a good ear and not through traditional studies. The first electronic music track I ever fell in love with was Snap!'s track, Rhythm Is A Dancer. It truly changed my life.

Till that point, I mostly listened to Israeli music and this track basically started it all. I got my first synthesizer at the age of twelve, it became my favourite instrument right away and still is the base for my musical works today. I started delving deeper into the production process and became fascinated with advanced technology and sound recording techniques."

Shoshan discovered club music in 1996 and was instantly hooked on artists such as Deep Dish, Paul

Oakenfold and DJ Tiësto. "I was fortunate enough to have a big brother who happened to be, to a larger extent, one of the pioneers of trance raves in Israel and he supplied me with the latest releases. At the age of sixteen, I recorded my first live album using my synthesizers. By some twist of fate, the album found its way to radio stations and many tracks received airplay.

> "The most thrilling memory was hearing Paul Oakenfold play five of my tracks in one night at a huge rave party in Israel."

"Soon after, I met Natali Dadon during a family trip to Jerusalem. The first time she sat and heard my music being played on cassette, she immediately loved it and has been the one who pushed me further. Natali had strong connections within the local nightlife scene in Jerusalem and somehow managed to hand a CD of my music to Paul Oakenfold while he was in Israel."

To his surprise, Oakenfold contacted them soon after. "About a year later, prior to his next visit in Israel, Natali and I decided to work on some new music, including Over Emotion, that we would play for him. Paul loved it right away and even included

Over Emotion in his set that same night.

Later on, we met the man who would become our manager and who then had ties with the major record labels out there. Lost Language loved the track, got us signed on their label and Natali and I started working under the LN Movement moniker. Over Emotion marks the first time when I felt I should not be afraid to pursue my dreams.

"Producing electronic music was a very unconscious process for me and felt really natural. I followed my heart and just loved making it. The most thrilling memory I have from this period was definitely hearing Paul Oakenfold play five of my tracks in one night at a huge rave party in Israel. I was only sixteen years old and it was so exhilarating to watch hundreds of people dance to my music. Looking back at this first encounter with trance music I realise that it laid the foundation for all my following musical endeavours."

MARCO V—*Simulated* (2001)
Marco Verkuylen, Netherlands

Just like his studio partner Benjamin Kuyten, Marco Verkuylen won his spurs in various music scenes before joining forces in the studio eventually. The pair did wonders in pushing back the limits of trance and techno and vice versa. With the release of Simulated under the guise of Marco V in 2001, the Dutchmen broke through to another level while establishing a fresh signature sound.

"I started off as a hip-hop DJ when I was fourteen years old and did all kinds of DJ-battles before getting interested in electronic music. At that time, there were a lot of mixing contests and battles where you could win money. With that money, I bought my first decks and, later on, a sampler. A little while later, I became a resident DJ at Danssalon, Eindhoven's largest club at the time and my interest initially turned to house music.

Soon after, I came across new hardcore and hard trance material from Germany, before taking the bend towards a combination of techno and trance. I released my first track in 1994 and knew from that moment that music was what I wanted to do for the rest of my life."

This is at Eindhoven's Danssalon, where they were both resident DJs, that Verkuylen met Benjamin Kuyten and the two would soon begin producing music together in the studio. This eventually led to a handful of releases under various monikers, including Southside Spinners and Marco V. Crucial in their career was a meeting with Dick de Groot, the A&R manager of Dutch powerhouse ID&T at the time, which would inflect the duo's soaring trajectory drastically.

"Dick told me he really liked my productions and wanted to start a new project for ID&T. I was mostly interested in producing a combination of techno and trance, which happened to be exactly what Dick was looking for.

"Back in the studio, Benjamin and I dedicated ourselves to working on new material. At some point, we were struggling with this short melody in a techno track that just didn't fit well. Dick happened to pass by the studio and felt this could be a hit, yet he suggested building the whole track around this melody. That is how the V.ision series and Simulated were born.

Trance was really big at the time and the techno feel of Simulated added something new to the game. Interestingly, people still want me to play that track live after all these years."

Although Verkuylen is glad as to how his musical career unfolded, he also feels that more opportunities could have helped him grow as an artist. "I am too much of a music lover and unfortunately not enough of a business or marketing man. That's something I could have done better. I guess I like to spend more time in the studio than on Facebook... Still, I am fortunate to have performed at some amazing trance parties back in the days.

My personal highlight was playing the main stage of Innercity in Amsterdam for the first time, in front of twenty thousand people. The energy in that massive hall was like nothing else I experienced before. There are still great trance events around nowadays, but not as many as before.

> "Trance was the main sound around the turn of the millennium: it turned into more of a niche scene, but that isn't necessarily a bad thing."

"Trance was the main sound around the turn of the millennium: it turned into more of a niche scene, but that isn't necessarily a bad thing. Production-wise I am back into tech-trance again, that's what gets me most excited these days. I also feel there is a new trance wave coming in the next couple of years."

MARK OTTEN—*Mushroom Therapy* (2003)
Mark Otten, Netherlands

Coming from a rich musical background, Mark Otten started his career as a drummer, though he also learned to play guitar and keyboard by himself. While his back catalogue remains fairly succinct with just a few records and remixes under his belt, his unique approach to sound—as examplified by Mushroom Therapy—is highly valued within the trance community.

"Music has been a vital part of my life since birth. I was literally a toddler beating on pots and pans and got put behind the drumkit of my father's band when I was about five years old. Also, my parents used to listen to a lot of rock and country music. I think my love for strong melodies originated then and there.

Some artists that grabbed my attention were Dire Straits, Fleetwood Mac and Mike Oldfield. Moonlight Shadow was my favourite track for years and I used to try and play the Tubular Bells theme on the piano as fast as possible. At one point, I fooled my best friend into thinking I could play it extremely fast by speeding up the recording—I guess the producer in me was already fiddling around back then.

"When my dad bought a small keyboard with sequencing options, everything changed. Even though there weren't a lot of cool sounds in there—and if I wanted a kick drum pattern for five minutes, I literally had to play that kick drum for five minutes—I was able to put my ideas down. The next step was my folks buying a PC. I linked up the keyboard to the PC and I was in heaven. It went even better when the first sound cards with sampling options became available on the market."

> "When I discovered trance, it was like stepping into a new world of hope and positivity and the scene reflected that feeling. To this day, this positive vibe is apparent in the scene."

Around the turn of the millennium, Otten started to make music with his friend Martijn van Oers. "While I was more of a nerdy producer, Martijn always had these original and commercially interesting ideas. I guess he wasn't very happy with the pace at which new tracks were coming along, so one day he suggested we do a little project called 'make a track in one day'. It worked surprisingly well and we only needed a couple more hours to finish the original version of Mushroom Therapy.

"However, I wanted to do my own take as well so I

started working on a remix as Lightscape, for which I used my guitar. It took me about three months to finish, partly due to the technical limitations of our computer and software. Eventually I ended up cutting the project up in ten different pieces and deleting unused sounds in different parts to make the computer run smoothly, after which I could glue those pieces together again."

Although some interest in the original version was shown, Mushroom Therapy didn't find a suitable home until two years later, in 2003. "I was attending a rehearsal of a friend's band, who happened to have a substitute guitar player that night, called Eller van Buuren.

We chatted for a bit and, luckily for me, Eller offered to take a CD with my music to present to his brother, Armin." About three days later, Otten received an email from Van Buuren. "Although there were multiple new tracks on that CD, the Lightscape remix of Mushroom Therapy turned out to be his favourite track."

Van Buuren opened his Essential Mix for BBC One with Mushroom Therapy and both versions were released on Armind soon after. Interestingly, Van Buuren still refers to Mushroom Therapy as the reason why he started Armada Music. "Armin's label Armind used to be part of United Recordings. United didn't feel Mushroom Therapy like he did, but Armin was determined to put it out, so it happened to be the final push he needed to start his own record company.

"When I discovered trance, it was like stepping into a new world of hope and positivity and the scene reflected that feeling. To this day, this positive vibe is apparent in the scene. Although most of it is now about the faster, uplifting trance—which, in all honesty, is not really my cup of tea—the atmosphere has not changed a lot.

If you look back in musical history, there have been a lot of new developments in music and styles coming out of technological advancement. I mean, the electrical guitar created a revolution and the same applies to the sampler. Trance was heavily linked to the release of a new type of synthesizer, with the Roland JP-8000 being the most important, as well as the rise of bedroom studios. I believe this could never have happened in any other era."

MICROGLOBE—*High On Hope* (1992)
Mijk van Dijk, Germany

Mijk van Dijk was one of the first artists to emerge from the early Berlin techno scene. Together with Harald Blüchel, Van Dijk coined the term 'trance' early on with their seminal compilation Tranceformed From Beyond. Soon after, High On Hope raised the bar for the techno-trance sound that quickly spread across continental Europe.

"I had been releasing hard techno under the moniker LoopZone since 1990, at a time when me and others were curious how hard and fast we could actually go with our music. Yet when I started DJing in 1992, I found out it was hard to mix my own music with other productions—which resulted in the production of more DJ-friendly tracks.

Since I used to be a bass player in bands, my tracks were always musical—sometimes too musical. Most productions turned out to be relatively complex and I kept using drum samples instead of Roland TR-808 or TR-909 drum machines. In fact, my main instruments were an Atari ST home computer and a sampler, along with a few cheap second-hand synths.

"To me, the trance sound as defined in Europe meant a melodious version of techno, often with lush pads, steady arpeggios and strong hooks. I understood it as a progression from the increasingly harder techno sound, by bringing back beauty to the beat. That sound fitted perfectly into the early nineties in Berlin—translating our feelings of new-found freedom and future-minded optimism into music.

During those early years, I also developed an interest in deeper, more melodic sounds, including the works of Detroit techno artists like Derrick May and Kevin Saunderson (especially his E-Dancer project) and the music that was then being played at clubs in Berlin like Planet. Tracks like Elbee Bad's New Age House, Format's Solid Session, GTO's Pure, Speedy J's Evolution and the original version of Age Of Love's The Age Of Love left a lasting mark on me."

Around that time, MFS Records launched their Trance Dance series and Van Dijk was introduced to Mark Reeder—who ran MFS—through Frontpage editor, Jürgen Laarmann. "After I joined the label, Mark asked Harald Blüchel (Cosmic Baby) and me to produce a Trance Dance remix compilation out of the existing MFS catalogue. This is how the idea for the Transformed From Beyond compilation came to be.

The release of Transformed From Beyond was quickly followed by my single High On Hope, released under the banner of Microglobe. The title referred to my dream that after the fall of the Berlin wall, mankind would finally enter an age of peace and mutual understanding.

"Interestingly, I didn't feel the single was that successful. The white labels of the Summer Mixes EP were a big hit around the Love Parade of 1992, but didn't come out until autumn of that same year due to restrictions that followed a change in the distribution process of MFS.

The release had to be marketed as a mini-album and sold at a higher price than a regular EP. As a result, not so many copies of the EP were sold, but it did pave the way for future projects and collaborations—such as the single Schöneberg as Marmion one year later.

Still, since High On Hope was included on a Tresor compilation, my music was brought to the attention of music enthusiasts the world over. I guess I still owe my ongoing popularity in Japan to this release. To me, High On Hope is a special track in many ways. However, it's too fast, too musical and too complex for today's club scene.

"If I were to give my definition of trance, it would be when a person moves into a repetitive state of groovy hypnosis, therefore losing all notion of time and space. This state of mind can be linked to tribal African dances, or reached by dancing to a monotonous electronic beat at a club or festival for hours on end.

I feel that the elements of trance as taken under this tribal perspective are still heavily linked to techno these days, just as they were in the early nineties. However, producers and DJs shy away from using the term, since it might associate their work to that particular era and aesthetic when trance became a commercial formula. I feel that is a shame, because trance as a concept is wonderful."

MINIMALISTIX—*Close Cover* (2001)
Peter Bellaert, Belgium

Belgian producer Peter Bellaert has been involved with electronic music ever since the early nineties. Out of the many projects he has taken part in, Minimalistix remains one of his most successful ventures, with several singles—often based on classical pieces from well-known composers such as Erik Satie and Wim Mertens—making it to the top of the charts. Close Cover went on to become one of the group's most widely appreciated works.

"My interest in music started at an early age: I think I was six years old when my mother took me with her on a regular basis to a friend of hers who owned a piano. The instrument really fascinated me—don't ask me why—but my mom never allowed me to touch it, as she feared I would break something.

When I was about nine years old, pop music such as Simple Minds, Art Of Noise, Pet Shop Boys, OMD, Frankie Goes To Hollywood, Duran Duran, U2 and more alternative music, from Kraftwerk to Pink Floyd, became of interest. And I started to use my father's old tape recorder to experiment with speed, noise and sound.

I was always intrigued by the sound of the music, how the sounds were created, how I could manipulate them. For example, I recorded vocals, instruments, random sounds and then put my fingers on the ribbon to control the speed in order to create special effects."

At the age of fifteen, artists like Anne Clark,

Front 242, Fad Gadget and The Cure piqued Bellaert's interest, as well as underground music such as new wave and early Detroit house. "Most of my friends were music lovers too: we bought records, recorded them on tape and then exchanged all our music. There was a continuous search for special sounds, especially for songs that weren't played on the radio but that were only to be heard in a number of select clubs (the underground scene). I was interested in many styles of music, but electronic sounds really intrigued and inspired me.

> "The name Minimalistix relates to the fact that Wim Mertens composed 'light' classical music, also known as minimalist music."

"When I turned eighteen years old, I bought my first keyboard, a Roland D-20, with my first savings. I didn't know how to read nor how to play music, but I was so obsessed with this keyboard that I used every spare moment to experiment with sound and noises. Later on, I bought my first sampler, a Roland W-30 and used the keyboard's sequencer to create patterns and songs. I was continuously trying to find out which electronic devices my favourite bands used to obtain their sound and that's how I actually started off."

As a result of his early productions and commercial success during the nineties, Bellaert started receiving a lot of demos, including one from Andy Vandierendonck, aka Steve Sidewinder. "Andy sent me a version of Struggle For Pleasure—originally a piece from the Belgian composer Wim Mertens. Around that time, the melody of this song was used in the television commercial of a Belgian telephone service provider. Andy suggested we make an electronic music version: I agreed and the project Minimalistix was born soon after.

Around that time, I also met Jo Casters from Roadrunner Arcade. We got along very well and instantly understood that cooperating was a logical step for us to take. Jo really believed in me and my musical abilities. He was very demanding when it came to sound: thanks to him and Kurt Dierckx I started training my ears to create the best possible sounds."

When working as part of Minimalistix, Belleaert chose to operate under the nickname Brian Koner. "Minimalistix may be considered a mixture of ideas from several people, with myself being the coordinator and producer. The project started with Andy, but later on Miguel Wittevrongel, Frederik Hulpia, Janus De Decker, Jo Casters, Pieter Loose, Els Mortelmans, Dave Lambert and Tom Snauwaert all got involved in the project at one point or another.

After creating a cover for Struggle For Pleasure,

we decided to cover Merten's composition Close Cover. It was better known and we also liked that theme a lot, so we turned Close Cover into a trance song as well. Many people seemed to like it and that single eventually turned into a major success."

Hence, Minimalistix became known as a group that mainly reshaped classical music into trance versions. "The name Minimalistix relates to the fact that Wim Mertens composed 'light' classical music, also known as minimalist music. His scores were not complicated: on the contrary, they were based on continuously repeating melodies. I guess this simplicity is part of the reason why Minimalistix became successful.

    The group's success brought me in touch with many interesting people—of which some became friends for life, while helping me become a better producer. This part of my musical career alone already made it worth the while. It's a wonderful feeling when you hear your own music on the radio and in clubs and to know that it is appreciated by others."

MR. SAM VS. FRED BAKER PRESENT AS ONE
—*Forever Waiting* (2003)
Samuel Paquet, France

Frenchman Samuel Paquet enveloped a niche for himself halfway the realms of techno and trance under the aliases of Mr. Sam and Mojado (together with Dimitri Andreas). He is credited as the artist with the most releases on DJ Tiësto's private label, Magik Muzik. Paquet's emotional piece Forever Waiting, produced together with Fréderic de Backer, set even higher standards for his ensuing productions.

"I grew up in a small city called Tourcoing in the north of France, surrounded by the disco music my mother used to listen to during the seventies. I soon became fascinated with sounds and the impact it could have on people—especially on myself. It was like a drug to me. I discovered electronic music around the late eighties when the Chicago house movement arrived in Europe: French Kiss by Lil' Louis was a revelation to me.

Prior to this, records were made by singers or bands that would perform on stage. With the emergence of house music, the records were suddenly coming from unheard producers making beats in their basement or bedroom. There were lots of mysteries as to how electronic music was made and the early nineties gave us the chance to experience a real revolution. It felt as if we were scientists who had just discovered some unknown continent: an indie movement, truly underground, that had nothing to do with the industry of today."

From then on, Paquet started buying records while working in a record shop called DIKI Records in Belgium, in the late nineties. "The shop had a fantastic reputation and many popular DJs dropped by to buy records. I was listening to every single vinyl that arrived: it was an obsession to me. I got asked to DJ at some local clubs and soon after, I was invited to play every weekend. It took me a few years, however, to begin composing my own music."

By 2002, Paquet left his record label N.E.W.S., the largest record company and distributor in the Benelux at the time, to take the leap into a new adventure. "As I was looking to find a new home for my music, I managed to set up a meeting with Arny Bink and Tijs Verwest from Black Hole Recordings. Funnily enough, Tiësto was officially crowned the world's number one DJ the day after our first meeting. Fréderic de Backer (aka Fred Baker) was my studio partner at the time. We felt that this was our only chance to make a good impression, so we had to come up with something special.

    I was inspired by the classy and timeless releases on Perfecto back then and had a strong idea on how I wanted the record to sound: epic, hypnotic and with a significant melody, being very emotional. We started with the groove, which were samples from a Jam & Spoon record, and added a snippet from a vocal session with Penny, the vocalist of Such Is Life by Rank 1. For the melody, we used a large string pad preset that we played as a single piano note instead of a chord change, making the track sound both epic and enigmatic. The track was eventually finished in just two days."

Since De Backer did not speak English, Paquet was running the business side of music. "I was sure this record was something special, so I was cheeky enough to go to the meeting with just this one track burned on a CDR. After an hour of discussion, we went to a small room in the back of the Black Hole office in Breda. I knew that this could become the most important moment of my musical life. Tijs was surprised that we only had a single track for him, but he played the track in its entirety.

> "I think mankind created music to heal our souls and offer us the opportunity to explore the emotions lying deep inside of us."

"When we played Forever Waiting, Tijs stood up at some point, beating the rhythm with his feet. When the breakdown came, he went wild and immediately wanted to sign it to his private record label Magik

Muzik. So we gave them the title, discussed the advance payment and finished the paperwork right there. Tijs is a true genius, musically gifted and certainly the DJ with the best ear in the electronic music game. It also makes me proud that I made this record with Fréderic, even though it happened to also be our last one together.

"To me, nothing beats the golden age of trance around the turn of the millennium: melodies, intentions, feelings, true stories behind the tracks, etcetera. Nowadays, trance music is more technical in terms of production and sounds, but suffers from a lack of creativity and spirit.

Yet, there is not a day I am not listening to music. I always enjoyed analysing pieces of music, to understand and discover the secret of its production. Unlike painting, sculpture or architecture, music is invincible and always appeared very mystical to me, like a magic trick or a myth. I think mankind created music to heal our souls and offer us the opportunity to explore the emotions lying deep inside of us. Music is definitely here to make us feel better."

NU NRG—*Dreamland* (2001)
Giuseppe Ottaviani, Italy

Embodying trance music's wild energy in both approach and output to perfection, Italian duo NU NRG, alias Giuseppe Ottaviani and Andrea Ribeca, quickly established themselves as spearheads of the trance movement by the early noughties. Their equally energetic and melodic take on the trance sound is further exemplified in their 2001-issued hit, Dreamland. Besides their main stream of releases as NU NRG, the pair also put out two singles as The Moon.

"I grew up listening to different kinds of music. Classical music was my biggest influence during my early youth, as my parents used to play classical records every day. Later on, I got hooked on bands like Queen and U2 (which I still am) as well as techno music, which led me to discover trance music later on. In fact, I got so deep into techno that I began to miss these orchestral melodies I used to hear in classical music. Suddenly, William Orbit's Adagio For Strings came out: it was the perfect link between my techno sound and classical music. That was the day I met trance music."

Soon after, Ottaviani met Andrea Ribeca through a common friend named Giacomo. "Andrea was already DJing in a proper club and I was just stepping into more progressive and trance music. He also had a very small studio and that was the first time I got to see a Nord Lead synthesizer and a Roland TR-909 drum machine.

 We became friends and together with Giacomo we decided to build a larger studio at Giacomo's house. A laptop wasn't enough back then, so it was a rather long journey. There was no Youtube to teach us how to do things. We still managed to set up a large mixing desk, lots of keyboards, speakers, a vocal booth and the first illegally downloaded software, as we were on a budget."

> "Trance proved to be a consistent genre throughout the past twenty years—and it will continue to be."

As the group started to produce their first tracks, they decided to name their collaborative project after a Roland MC-505 sound bank: NU NRG. "While Andrea and I made our way into the musical path we both believed in the most, Giacomo took the bend towards more commercial-friendly horizons than trance. NU NRG turned into a two-man group and we released our first record called Energyzer on a small label from Rome called Synthetic. We also started playing together and got to play gigs in local clubs."

 Although starting out as a DJ act, the duo instantly fell in love with the live experience. "Bringing all the hardware on stage to perform live was just so exciting, but also unstable as hell. We worked more with that label, making new tracks and new EPs and when everything was underway I then had to leave for a mandatory period in the Italian army.

I used the army to my advantage: normally people had to spend twelve months in the army without pay, so I decided to take part in an entrance examination to enter the army as a lieutenant and get paid decent wages. I succeeded and used nearly all my money to build my home studio."

Born in Ottaviani's new studio, the duo's hit single Dreamland was initially released on Synthetic but unexpectedly came into the hands of Paul Van Dyk. "Paul really wanted to sign us on his Vandit record label and offered us to play at the infamous Love Parade in Berlin, which proved to be the beginning of my new career.

I was still working in the army at the time and actually planned to stay put as it offered me very good money and I was enjoying my work so much that I became an instructor. I had a group of people to teach while having fun together, shooting at targets and playing as you do in paintball. However, I never realised the real implications of my job until 9/11. After that, everything changed and I suddenly realised that I could never shoot at actual people instead of the wood-made targets we were then taking aim at, so I ended my army career.

NU NRG was doing extremely well from that

moment onwards and our popularity soared rapidly, especially after Dreamland broke through into the German charts. Lots of gigs around the world, playing for the biggest brands and other events followed, up until the day when, unfortunately, we split up. I had to start again. It happened to be the starting point of my solo career."

As Ottaviani's career steadily continues, he believes trance will not go out of fashion anytime soon. "The thing about trance is that it didn't come up for a couple of years and then disappeared. In fact, trance proved to be a consistent genre throughout the past twenty years—and it will continue to be. But one cannot expect today's trance to sound exactly the same as in the early days. Technology has evolved and the way music is being written is obviously different now. Yet, the nature of trance music is still the same. Changing your dress will make you look a bit different, but it won't change who you are."

PARAGLIDERS—*Paraglide* (1993)
Oliver Lieb, Germany

Frankfurt-born Oliver Lieb is one of the most prolific electronic music producers of his time, having collated hundreds of releases over the years, plus a host of choice remixes for world-renowned acts such as Faithless, Moby, Snap! and Yello. Although Lieb created some of the most decisively defining tracks within the circle of trance, his back catalogue also includes successful forays in electronic genres as diverse as EBM, hardcore, house and techno. The Paragliders project (in collaboration with Torsten Stenzel) provided an early projection of Lieb's musical potential, which later found incarnations in various guises.

"From my early teens onwards, the radio played an essential part in the development of my taste in music. I started listening to all kinds of music: everything that was being played on the radio, as well as music that friends liked. When I was around fourteen years old I started playing bass, thanks to a great teacher from the United States. He motivated me to practice several hours a day to get better. From that moment on, listening to the radio became even more important to me and took up a lot of my time."

Lieb went on to play the bass in multiple funk and soul bands. That said, he often left these bands before they got to meet with success. "A few years later, however, I gave up playing in bands when the equipment became a bit cheaper and I could do everything myself.

I was listening to Pink Floyd, Yello, Kraftwerk, funk music and some of the early so-called EBM stuff during my 'bass' period. Yet hip-hop, rap and the early acid and house movements became more appealing to me when I got into the process of making electronic music. There were just so many genres to discover and I wanted to dig into all of them. It became clear to me that I wanted to dedicate my life to this and luckily, I have been able to make music full-time since 1993."

Lieb released his first record, System, as Force Legato in 1989—a studio project he had with Torsten Fenslau, who also ran Abfahrt Records. The single triggered impressive reactions worldwide and almost made it into the German charts. In the following years, Lieb's releases would go on to cover all possible corners of the electronic music spectrum, from downtempo and chill-out to hard experimental techno and trance.

"One of these projects was Paragliders, together with Torsten Stenzel. We had met not long before and decided to collaborate, but finding time was always a bit of a problem. So we were able to create the A-side tracks of the first two Paragliders records together, including Paraglide, but since we wanted to release these tracks as soon as possible, I created the B-side tracks and remixes myself."

Meanwhile, Lieb's monikers Spicelab and The Ambush

became closely associated with Sven Väth's seminal label, Harthouse, a platform designed to harbour and promote the German DJ and producer's favourites. This long-term collaboration gave birth to eight extended players and three albums over a time span of just two years.

"These projects did particularly well and soon took up all my focus. It actually took me a while to realise I wanted to continue the Paragliders project as well, so I did a few records on my own and some on different record labels."

Out of the dozen different aliases under his belt, Lieb couldn't be more unfazed as to the styles of music to which his name has been attached. "I don't care about genres so much, I just created different projects, each pushing a different sound: from hardcore to more melodic, experimental and chill-out works. Being part of this early movement and doing something completely new back then—way before people invented names for whatever specific genre they were hearing, was just great when I think about it today.

I also believe that the original trance sound was fresher, original and not that much about sales and money: basically the whole scene was in a better condition. To me, Children by Robert Miles basically marked the beginning of the end of trance. Back then, the audience in clubs was more open: people went to parties to hear something new or didn't really know what to expect. That attitude changed completely."

Svenson & Gielen at Mysteryland, 2001 © ID&T

PUSH—*Universal Nation* (1998)
Mike Dierickx, Belgium

Belgian producer Mike Dierickx, real name Dirk Dierickx, has been one of the most productive artists within the trance domain. Having started DJing under the alias of DJ Mike, Dierickx went on to release hundreds of tracks in a host of guises from the early nineties on, including Absolute, Liquid Overdose, M.I.K.E., Plastic Boy and Solar Factor. If there is one single track to highlight from Dierickx's back catalogue, it most certainly is Universal Nation—the single that made him a favourite amongst DJs worldwide.

> "The recognition and status that Universal Nation holds in the industry is unbeatable."

"When I was very young, I loved buying records at the local vinyl shop, then rushing home and playing them for hours. I fell in love with the thought of how one could make or create music and began recording mixtapes myself afterwards.

Growing up in the eighties, the synth-pop era with bands like Soft Cell, Fad Gadget, Front 242 and Depeche Mode had a heavy influence on my musical preferences. The genre was centred around the use of synthesizers and drum machines, so that's where my interest in technology came from. It was then that I noticed how music could bring people to a state of ecstasy, making them feel both euphoric and emotional at the same time. I loved that."

With the drum machine and the 8-bit sampler he was then in possession of, fourteen-years-old Dierickx locked himself in his bedroom and started fiddling with hardware, tape recorders and vinyl. When dance music came around in the early nineties, he moved in that direction.

"When my initial plan to become a football player was set aside, I handed my first demo to USA Import Records in Antwerp—a well-known record store and label at the time. My first release under the moniker Vision Act saw the light in 1992."

The breakthrough came with Universal Nation under his Push moniker in 1998. Produced in just four hours on a Wednesday afternoon, the track eventually turned into a hit more than a year after its initial release, when DJ Tiësto picked up on Dierickx's more melodic works. "Tiësto took it to another level, he was the biggest supporter of my early music. The recognition and status that Universal Nation holds in the industry is unbeatable. Universal Nation is me—it's my baby. It keeps me going every day. I feel blessed."

According to Dierickx, his music was born out of combining elements from different genres and technology at hand, such as synths, samplers and drum machines. "I like to bring all sorts of different musical elements together under various aliases, each of which has its own identity. So many aliases are associated with a particular sound that I have trouble naming them all sometimes. Basically all my tracks are inspired by an event or situation, or just emerge out of the blue."

Consequently, Dierickx is a firm believer that there is much more to trance than just its musical reference. "Trance was around way before it made its way into the club circuit. It's a feeling that triggers our emotions on a much deeper level. I notice that people want to be touched again by music."

RALPHIE B—*Massive* (2001)
Ralph Barendse, Netherlands

The steady-going success of Ralph Barendse's releases coincided with that of the Dutch trance scene's golden age, right at the beginning of the noughties. When it comes to the big-room branch of trance's floriferous family tree, Ralphie B's aptly named hit, Massive, has proven to be a knockout argument in any discussion invoking the genre's unmatched epic potential with its mix of spacious pads, thrilling breaks and high-intensity programming.

"I have had no musical education nor followed any courses, so I cannot read notes or play an instrument. Instead, my background lies in playing my mother's electronic organ—those with pre-programmed rhythms such as bossa nova, polka, waltz as well as a small synthesizer sounds section.

When I grew older, I bought myself a Yamaha PSR keyboard. And every few years I bought a new, larger keyboard until I eventually got into buying synthesizers such as the Yamaha CS1X and AN1X. After some time, I also got myself a Soundblaster sound card and started making dance tracks on a PC, with these so-called tracker programs. This led me to toy with samples for the first time.

"Around that time, I used to buy records and CDs at a shop in Dordrecht. The owner, Jayant Edoo, also had his own studio and record label. After some time, I gave him a demo CD with a couple of my tracks. One of those tracks ended up being released on Deal Records.

A few Alpha Breed releases later, in 2001, I developed a desire to collaborate with In Trance We Trust. I knew Black Hole, the label's mother company, from listening to DJ Tiësto's tracks and compilations and got to visit their Magik store in Breda on a regular basis.

"Trance music was still under the radar back then: DJs and radio stations were mainly playing house music, happy hardcore and gabber, while my focus was rather on the German and Belgian sound. I used to listen to rave records from labels like Low Spirit, Superstition and more early trance records on Bonzai. Also, I used to go out in Belgian club and visited festivals like Mayday in Germany, which influenced my music heavily."

Barendse wrote his arguably most successful record in 2001, right after he acquired an Access Virus synthesizer. "Back then I used to listen to a lot of DJ sets from Paul Oakenfold, which got me infected with the UK sound—having a more progressive edge, crazy sounds, techy beats and acid lines. My new Roland JP-8000 synthesizer had all these crazy sounds within easy reach and the track turned out to be more progressive and less euphoric than anything I had ever made before. I guess the track has an interesting hook and melody. It wasn't cheesy compared to a lot of tunes back then.

After finishing the track, I chose to call it Massiva

and planned to release it under my Alpha Breed moniker. I asked Deal Records to send it to Black Hole, but the studio I had a contract with remastered my track and sent it over as Ralphie B—Massive, as they thought Massiva was a typing-error.

"Eventually I received a call from Black Hole's A&R manager, William Commandeur, who told me on the phone he liked the track but it did not really lift off. According to him, it was missing a climax. Disappointed as I was, I refused to change anything on the track. Instead, we sent the demo to Warner Music, whose A&R manager was Maykel Piron back then, now head of Armada Music. Although we had worked together in the past, Warner also rejected the track.

My publisher at the time, Pieter van Bodegraven, was also doing the publishing for Tiësto and other Black Hole artists. He was convinced that Massive was a great track and brought it on CD to one of his meetings with Tiësto. Tijs loved it and I got a phone call from Black Hole on my birthday that they had changed their mind and wanted to sign it. The white label floated into Tiësto's sets only weeks later and got ID-ed as a new Cygnus X track due to its similar chord lines with Superstring.

"Massive was released on In Trance We Trust that summer and, since it did so well in terms of sales, the track was also licensed to Paul van Dyk's Vandit Records, as well as Data Records. Paul van Dyk himself even made an edit, but that version unfortunately never found its way out.

It still makes me proud when people send a message about the memories my tracks give them, or when young people just discovered my music through remixes. However, there is also a downside to making tracks that gain lots of success. Each new track I make ends up being invariably compared to the classics I made before. That can be frustrating. I might never have a bigger impact than with those tracks from the 2001-2003 era."

A couple of years into the new millennium, money was flowing in the music business and releasing a hit meant tidy sums landing on the bank account. With the sales from his first releases as Ralphie B and Midway, Barendse was even able to buy himself a brand new car. "I also received many remix offers for artists such as Dario G and Solarstone. It was normal to pay huge amounts of money for remixes, generally around two thousand to four thousand Pounds.

However, I still felt like a bit of an outsider, as I always considered music as a hobby. I kept my day job in IT management, even though I was making music at night and DJ-ed all around the world while raising a family with kids. Although I tried it, it does not work for me to make music templates. I usually make a track and don't go into the studio for a while again."

RIVA—*Stringer* (2001)
René ter Horst, Netherlands

Drawn together by their common love for the house music movement of the early nineties, the discography of Dutchmen René ter Horst and Gaston Steenkist counts over four hundred releases spanning across the widest array of electronic music genres, issued under a variety of monikers including Chocolate Puma, Jark Prongo and The Good Men. As Riva, the duo made fame in the trance domain with their Balearic to-be-classic Stringer.

"When I started listening to music, my first inspirations were artists experimenting with synthesizers, such as Prince, Depeche Mode and Nitzer Ebb. Later on, early house producers such as Derrick May, DJ Pierre, Todd Terry, The Orb and Marshall Jefferson captivated me.

While my interest in electronic music began in the eighties, these first house records, which were made completely with drum computers, sequencers and synthesizers, were exactly what I wanted to create. An artist album based on only one kind of drum kit or piano sounded boring to me. I needed to hear all those different, alien electronic sounds.

I did some research on gear and found that I needed a lot of tools, like a drum programmer, sequencer, keyboard, sampler, synthesizers, etcetera. And of course, I didn't have the money to buy all those items. Then one day, while I was passing through some music store, something completely new was presented to me: a Roland W-30 workstation, which was an all-in-one sequencer, sampler, keyboard and synthesizer. It soon became my first piece of gear.

"A bit later on, I had a radio show where we played house music only, which was a novelty at that time, and asked listeners to send us demos. There was one demo that I really liked, from Gaston Steenkist, so I invited him to the studio. Soon after that we made our first track together as Tomba Vira, called La Mandarina.

Since then, we never stopped making music together. We've always enjoyed dabbling in various styles of music and at that time it was common for producers to try and release a maximum of records a month. That's how we came to releasing so many diverse records under distinct aliases. When we made Stringer, which was again a different style of music to us, we felt the need to come up with a new moniker, Riva.

"Interestingly, we've never been huge fans of trance music: the feel of the grooves and beats of most trance records out there were not quite our cup of tea. Hence, we didn't know much about the genre but just wanted to make a trance record we would like ourselves.

We had some fun in the studio and created this trance record that, in our opinion, had the right groove and feel. Stringer was created in a few hours and we completely forgot about it until months later, when we played some DAT tapes to the A&R manager of United Recordings. One track that really stood out for him was Stringer.

Hence, the record got released under our new moniker and this unassuming instrumental track became a big hit on Ibiza. We heard that a lot of the big trance DJs loved it. Eventually, Stringer got signed by London Records and before we knew it, we had Dannii Minogue featured as a singer and the single ended up number two in the UK charts."

The success met by Stringer was soon to be followed by a steady stream of remix requests. "We had a lot of fun doing that but weren't after having a trance career. It was more of a fun side-project which we loved doing as producers.

However, the record means a lot to us, even though we made it just for fun: it was born from our hearts and we still think it's a bloody good record. As such, I do think trance fits perfectly into the timeframe of that era, but the same goes for any musical style. As with any genre that gets to be so popular, trance has known its climax and been through some kind of comedown. Still, it will never fully disappear."

SANDER KLEINENBERG—*My Lexicon* (2000)
Sander Kleinenberg, Netherlands

Sander Kleinenberg breezed into the late progressive game without further ado in 2000, when his single My Lexicon made a direct hit in the hearts of clubbers. He is also credited as one of the first artists to have incorporated digital video (VJing) in his concerts.

"Hip-hop was my first love in the mid-eighties and logically became a gateway into electronic music for me. Back then, hip-hop was much more of a movement and not only connected to rap. A lot of music had electronic influences and house music was also part of the urban movement that came from the United States. Depeche Mode, Stevie Wonder and Michael Jackson where also some of my earlier influences."

Kleinenberg started DJing at a local bar in 1987 at the age of fifteen, where he used to play a variety of music, running the gamut from rock to dance music, via a wealth of other styles. "By 1992, electronic developments made it a little bit more accessible to make music yourself. As a result, I was able to invest in equipment and my first releases soon followed on labels like Wonka Beats, Superstition and Strictly Rhythm.

"In the late nineties, I fell in love with British progressive house. Especially the music of artists like Underworld, The Chemical Brothers, Leftfield and Sasha caught my attention. They all became sources of inspiration for me and I started to make more tracks within that particular field. My Lexicon came as the result of me exploring that sound and was luckily picked up by the biggest DJs in the world. Back then, Pete Tong was a strong supporter of progressive house, so he selected My Lexicon and signed it to his label FFRR."

From that moment on, the snowball effect was on and Kleinenberg's international career was catapulted to higher spheres. "I think I was able to capture human emotion in my records, but the reality is that records are not successful in their own right. A hit record needs to perfectly capture time and space and be embraced by people. Therefore, you can only be humble when it happens to you. My Lexicon was without question the most important record of my career. It made my status evolve from a local DJ into an international artist almost overnight. When it happens, you hardly have any moment to let it sink in."

As the music industry entered a new phase with the new millennium's arrival, the parameters of Kleinenberg's early success were thrown over in the most dramatic way possible.

"The benefits that came with being upfront and maintaining healthy connections vanished with the introduction of the internet's democratic way of distributing content. The principal consequence in the emergence of this transparent and fan-driven world was that big shift in the market's overall approach. DJs had to learn to be more responsive towards the needs of the audience and became less inclined to dictate the crowd.

"It would be too lazy and abstruse, however, to try pinpointing the differences in the way we have consumed and marketed music over the last fifteen years, or the way it has affected the global positioning and business models of DJs and artists. A good record or a great idea, combined with a healthy work ethic, will never be replaced by these new instruments: you still need to use them in an effective way.

Adding to that, I think trance music was and still is, rather timeless. The big difference between now and then is our relation to time on a dance floor. Nowadays, the attention span of the crowd has moved back to what it was in the late eighties. People want something new every three or four minutes.

"Around the turn of the millennium, records could be ten minutes or longer and people would totally go with it. But just like everything else, these things tend to go in and out of fashion. This might have to do with the fact that electronic music has become so popular that it's now harder to find a group of people willing to commit as much time and focus to the experience."

SIGNUM—*First Strike* (2001)
Ron Hagen, Netherlands

Dutch duo Pascal Minnaard and Ron Hagen made a name for themselves through a string of powerful releases and remixes as Signum. Their notoriously funky productions quickly became a favourite amongst DJs, with First Strike making for the duo's flagship track.

"I've been involved with music since the age of twelve, when I began learning the keyboard on my own. I also soaked in as much knowledge as possible regarding jazz/fusion music. When I finally got a GEM keyboard workstation, I'd go to the library in my spare time to read books about MIDI, arrangements and reading notes. Eventually I managed to buy an Atari ST home computer, which kickstarted my musical development.

"Pascal and I met in high school and as he was also heavily involved with music production we would hang out at each other's place, bring our equipment and just jam away, playing tunes and experimenting with sampling and synthesizers. We both definitely influenced each other musically.

We lost touch for some time, after I changed schools, but we ran into one another again in 1997. Pascal had just delivered a tape with a couple of unfinished tracks to a newly established record company called BPM Dance that was based out of our hometown, Zoetermeer. The owners, Freek Fontein and Randy Katana, immediately handed him a record deal. Pascal encouraged me to follow suit and I was soon signed to the label too."

Shortly after, the duo merged all their equipment and moved into a studio space next to BPM Dance. "We received an advance payment from our publisher, which enabled us to buy even more and better gear. Countless hours were spent in that studio, experimenting, learning and just building loads of tracks. There were no boundaries, except for limitations of knowledge and equipment. And as the internet wasn't really a thing yet, our only influences were the tracks that actually did get released on wax.

The BPM Dance building was filled with studios. One of the rooms was occupied by Mac Zimms—someone we always looked up to, as his productions were way ahead of his time. He made more club-house-oriented material, which accidentally influenced our approach towards trance. I loved the bounciness of these house rhythms, which I wasn't able to find in most trance releases back then. Consequently, later Signum tracks and remixes always embraced that bouncy rhythm, combined with more melodic elements.

"After our first two singles, What Ya Got 4 Me and Coming On Strong, remix requests just flooded in. Every major label seemed to be wanting that same Signum sound. Yet, at that moment we had gone a bit more experimental and remixes were rejected. So we felt forced to repeat that same trick over and over again—which killed our creativity."

Their next record, First Strike, was born out of frustration. "We wanted to do something completely different, while still incorporating that melodic feel of a Signum track. If we managed to do this with a release of our own, chances were that we would get more freedom with our remixes—and it proved to work. The main drum loop of First Strike was ripped from a vinyl record, while we also sampled some small percussion bits from Dutch band Slagerij van Kampen. First Strike was, for us, the transition to a more mature sound.

"Following our releases and remixes, we soon received booking requests from different parts of the world. However, we had no idea how to DJ. So we started practising every single night for a good year, until we were sure enough to mix properly. Our first actual bookings took place around the turn of the century, including a three-hour set at the legendary Gatecrasher club in Sheffield. That opportunity turned my life upside down—and still does, actually."

"When Pascal moved to Norway in 2007, we literally flipped a coin to decide which one of us would take care of future DJ gigs—which happened to be me. Since then, I've been performing as well as producing individually as Signum—while also having taken a five-year break in between. Looking back, my career in music has brought me amazing highs, but also very deep lows. It took some soul-searching and hard obstacles to move on, but eventually I was brought to the right place again."

SOLARSTONE—*Seven Cities* (1999)
Richard Mowatt, United Kingdom

Born in Ireland but raised up in Wales, Richard Mowatt is generally considered a founding father of the Balearic trance sound, which—as its name suggests—carries in its heart the sun-dazed, balmy character of the clubbers' paradise that is Ibiza. Though not intended as such in the first place, Seven Cities became a flagship theme for a whole generation of trance lovers, as well as one of Mowatt's most acclaimed pieces.

"As a teenager, I would tune in to Radio Luxembourg and Jeff Young's Big Beat show to hear early acid house music. I was hooked. Finally here was a type of music I could make despite having no classical music skills. My main influences on wanting to produce music were the Pet Shop Boys. I always loved their combination of a unique trademark sound and their approach to pop art."

Trance came up on Mowatt's radar in the mid-nineties through the likes of Eye Q and his growing interest in production soon led him to acquire a Casio SK1—bought by his mother when he was fifteen years old. "This Casio could record four samples using the line-in connection and had a rudimentary sequencer. I wrote all my earliest stuff on that. A couple of years later, I was able to buy a Korg M1. That was when I made the decision to build a life around music. I did various low-paid jobs to support my hobby including factory work, barman and body-piercing, but eventually I began earning enough to make it my profession.

"Pretty much the entire period that followed was spent in the studio. We were this big gang of mates who all went out clubbing, smoking weed, taking pills. Most of my friends were into techno—as opposed to the trance scene, so we would go to events like Atomic Jam and House Of God in Birmingham. I picked up a lot of production tricks from those events actually and injected elements like how a track could lock you in when 'under the influence'. Then after the club, everyone would pile back to someone's house where the afterparty would begin."

His collaborative venture with Andy Bury and Sam Tierney, Solar Stone, soon monopolised his time and energy. The project, born from the ashes of their previous one, Space Kittens, was incepted in Birmingham in 1997 and later renamed to Solarstone.

When Tierney left the band due to differences, Bury and Mowatt went on to operate under various aliases including Young Parisians, Liquid State and Z2. The pair's career took substantial steps towards further mainstream recognition with the release of Seven Cities—a Balearic anthem fusing an atmospheric breakdown with uplifting choruses and catchy guitar riffs. "I wrote the chords, bassline and lead melody one day after being stuck in a rut for a while. It was one of those tracks which came fully formed one night when I was asleep. I awoke one morning and there it was."

Seven Cities was Solarstone's third collaboration with Hooj Choons. "The relationship with Hooj Choons was great and terrible at the same time: 'Red' Jerry [Dickens] was so passionate about his label and there was a great team working there, but he was also very 'on it' in terms of what was going to happen next.

Initially, when Hooj Choons got the demo they considered the breakdown to be too long—big breakdowns were very rare in those days. Yet, either one of us or Jerry gave a DAT to Paul Oakenfold, which he played at Cream in Liverpool: the rest is history."

> "Trance is only bound to a period by people who have moved on musically, stopped going out, had families—those who left the scene."

Inevitably, the global success of Seven Cities was caught in the even more global upward spiral enjoyed by more commercial, 'Ibiza-oriented' trance music. "To me, Seven Cities was just another release at that time. I thought it was a good record, don't get me wrong, but its status has been assumed by the people who heard it at a particular time in their lives—the Ibiza connection, the general explosion of trance at that time. It was a matter of it being the right moment for the track. It means a lot to many people and I still love it, but it is not the most important thing I have done in my career."

When covering the genre as a whole, Mowatt happens to be a passionate purveyor of 'his' scene. "Trance is only bound to a period by people who have moved on musically, stopped going out, had families—those who left the scene. To people within the scene, it is a different story altogether. There was a point when I was becoming disillusioned with the trance scene. But by now, trance has never been so exciting to me. There is a new generation of fans now. To them, trance is something new.

While the sound keeps evolving, the same three things speak to people: groove, melody and emotion. Every time I get sent or hear a great trance record, it is just as good a feeling as it was twenty years ago. And with the trance scene being so fresh and full of new talent, it is never dull. Nothing can replace the feeling of rapture that trance music awakens in people."

TASTEXPERIENCE—*Summersault* (1997)
Russell Barker, United Kingdom

TasteXperience was a British music group consisting of Nigel Palmer, Richard Cornish and Russell Barker. The trio has prided itself on the uniqueness of its sound, built out of a vast amount of real instruments used within the recording process. Their breakthrough came with Summersault in 1997—a beautiful trip down memory lane rife with warm, heavenly chords.

"Our group started off as a guitar-and-drums band with influences from sixties bands such as The Beatles, Northern soul and Motown music. We got into the first wave of electronic music during the mid-eighties, using sequencers and drum machines which progressed to Atari 1040ST home computer and AKIA samplers. In the early nineties, we started going clubbing and were into bands such as The Orb, Massive Attack and Innocence.

At the time we were managed by Tom Watkins—known for his work with Pet Shop Boys, Bros and East 17—and had a successful debut track called Frustration in the United States in 1992. As such, we were hanging out with people like Moby and Sasha while touring Florida. Upon returning to the United Kingdom, we signed to Polydor in 1993 and released the club hit Free, which gained us credits within the domestic music industry."

During the mid-nineties, the group used to hang out

in clubs like The Cross, Camden Place, Whirly Gig, Limelight, Bagleys and Ministry Of Sound. "We did get lots of feelings of love and unity from the clubbers. At this point we also started travelling to Southeast Asia: swinging in hammocks, listening to chill-out music and dancing at these full-moon parties. A mixture of these experiences led to the writing of Summersault, which was recorded in our studio in Stambridge in 1997."

Recorded in just one night, the three men didn't finish the track until eight AM the next day. "When Nigel and I went to our car to drive home, it didn't start so we had to phone a maintenance service. We still had a two-hour journey ahead of us, Summersault was melting in our heads and this lorry driver kept talking non-stop. I'll never forget that moment."

> "There is a godly presence and energy with this kind of music that connects you with a higher being."

The success of Summersault soon followed, after a friend of the group who had been given a copy of the record passed it on to Paul Oakenfold, who then started using it as the opening track in his sets. "Ben Cherill from Manifesto heard the track on BBC Radio

One and loved it straight away. We eventually signed it to Manifesto, reached number one in the UK dance charts and Summersault appeared on many compilation albums."

One of Barker's fondest memories was of hearing everyone play their track on repeat at the large-scale festival Creamfields. "Every tent we went in, they were playing Summersault! Even when we left and turned on BBC Radio One, there it was again. Although we had released many records before, Summersault really caught the imagination and feelings of the time for many people.

I think it's a spiritual and melodic song that takes the listener to a special place, time and time again. Summersault was the icing on the cake and opened many doors for us, including our signing to Black Hole and finally, Perfecto.

"Trance is a universal language and the euphoric feeling of listening and dancing to trance music doesn't compare to that of any other forms of music. To me, there is a godly presence and energy with this kind of music that connects you with a higher being. Trance music will always be around as long as people make music and are in the need of escaping to another world."

THE THRILLSEEKERS—*Synaesthesia* (1999)
Steve Helstrip, United Kingdom

Then living in Chipping Norton, United Kingdom, Steve Helstrip got his start in the world of trance music while working for a computer games developer, Manic Media. In parallel to producing music as The Thrillseekers, the alias under which he composed the global hit Synaesthesia, Helstrip also released music as En-Motion, Insigma, Rapid Eye and Hydra.

"In my early teens I was a big fan of Erasure, which led me to discover Depeche Mode through the connection with keyboard player and songwriter Vince Clarke. The early Depeche Mode albums became staple listening for me, along with other synth-pop artists such as The Human League, Pet Shop Boys and New Order.

I had a keyboard at home since the age of eleven and progressed onto buying synthesizers and other electronic music gear during my teens. I spent my youth playing in bands and creating my own synth-pop tracks. Whilst studying classical music and composition, I formed a pop group called The Flood and we even signed to ZTT—home of artists such as Frankie Goes To Hollywood, Grace Jones and Roy Orbison—for one single. There has never been anything else than music that I've been so passionate about."

Though Helstrip had already been creating electronic music during his high school years in the eighties, it wasn't until 1998 that he came across Offshore by Chicane. "That was a life-changing track for me and happened to be the turning point for my musical direction. I loved the track's simplicity—essentially being just a two-note melody—and the emotion it conveyed over its chord progression. I knew I wanted to write something in that genre, although with a view to making a more club-friendly mix with more energy.

Next came the title, Synaesthesia, and thoughts of how to convey its meaning towards a musical context. The main melody came about really quickly, probably in less than thirty minutes. It is just three notes, like many of the best musical hooks are, but they play over an evolving chord progression which really brings the track to life.

"The actual production of the track took much longer, though. I literally spent six months perfecting all the different parts and layers to the best of my abilities, knowing that I had a potential hit on my hands. Of course, back then, technology was pretty limited and I had to make do with a very basic home studio at the time.

After I wrote Synaesthesia, my manager took the track to a few record labels to see who might be interested in releasing it. Neo snapped it up immediately for one thousand Pounds, which seemed like a decent advance payment at the time. A few weeks later, Positiva came back with an offer of sixty thousand Pounds. You can probably imagine how that went down!

The track was played by most known DJs at the time and was even used in the club scene of the movie 51st State. Synaesthesia became the defining start of my trance career and it could not have got off better, really.

"That period between 1998 and 2003 was the golden era of trance music. I would come across five to six stand-out records every week, each with their own identity. You could spot a Paul van Dyk record a mile away and likewise for many other producers. There are still some amazing trance records being made today, but they are few and far between by comparison. Most tracks just sound very much alike.

However, trance will never be bound to a period. It will further evolve and is currently enjoying a resurgence. While many of the pioneers of trance have jumped ship to follow the latest trends, I've stayed in the scene since the beginning. It's what I live for."

THREE DRIVES ON A VINYL—*Greece 2000* (1997)
Erik de Koning, Netherlands

Three Drives, also known as Three Drives on a Vinyl, was founded by Erik de Koning and Ton van Empel at the end of the nineties. The duo also operated under the monikers Fate Federation, Tangled Universe, Love Foundation, Positiv, Force Full and Legal Traders. As Three Drives, the duo was responsible for the 1997-issued Ibiza anthem Greece 2000.

"I stumbled upon songs from Jean-Michel Jarre in my early teens and started listening to electronic music in my bedroom via pirate radio stations. One of these channels was then playing Italo music, which gave me an amazing feeling as I had never heard anything like that before. From that moment on I began listening to this type of music continuously, both in my car and at home.

Then I started working at a record store called Mid-Town, which had also set up a record label at an early stage. I was already DJing on a regular basis, so it felt natural for me to move to music production as well. Wouldn't it be amazing to make your own track and be able to play it yourself in a club?

I started to ask my boss if I could have a look in the studio, but for some reason this never happened. At some point I couldn't wait any longer: with the rest of my money I bought a Casio FZ1 sampler and an Alesis MMT8 sequencer. From that moment on, I was so focused on producing music that I literally worked on it day and night."

Between 1995 and 1997, De Koning built his own studio in the infamous Dolhuis recording studios in Dordrecht. "I had been releasing a lot of hardcore music, but started evolving towards club music as the general interest in hardcore vanished. I was renting a studio room from Lucien Foort and Ton van Empel used to visit him regularly.

Soon after, Ton and I decided to start working together on Mondays and Tuesdays. We made a lot of tracks under different monikers. I remember that one time when I was playing around with sounds and melodies, Ton overheard a melody and pressed the record button: the melody of Greece 2000 was born and it took us only three days to finish the track."

Still, the destiny of Greece 2000 wasn't written in advance. "Nobody seemed to like the track and Massive Drive released it solely as a favour to us. The initial sales were bad and nobody played the track until Judge Jules picked it up on BBC Radio One—one year after its release.

After that, everything went very fast and we ended up in the top ten of the UK singles chart. The trance scene was growing rapidly and events were evolving to a higher level all over Europe, largely due to the efforts of Armin, Ferry and Tiësto. Greece 2000 fitted perfectly in that moment: it just seemed to mix the right sounds and melodies."
De Koning recalls a particularly memorable moment

following the release. "We had a live performance of Greece 2000 scheduled on a German TV network called Viva, which had fourteen million viewers. We were so new to this and had no clue how to behave. Also, we didn't speak German, so we had a guide with us to translate the questions from the host and the viewers. After that, I've never been scared to perform anymore."

Over the course of years, De Koning's love for trance hasn't changed. "If we could travel back in time to the year 1998, I would do things exactly the same as I did back then. Maybe trance is not as popular as it was before 2005—which was, to me, the best time for trance music. Fans grew older, tastes changed and the next generation doesn't enjoy trance as much. Yet, the sound of trance is still timeless to me.

Making a living out of music production has become more difficult, though. There are so many new talents out there who struggle to survive. I hope they continue and give the world new influences so that the genre evolves even more across the coming decade."

TUKAN—*Light A Rainbow* (2000)
Søren Weile, Denmark

A most representative exponent of quality peak-time trance, Light A Rainbow—the debut single of Danish duo Lars Frederiksen and Søren Weile as Tukan—became a global hit single around the turn of the millennium. Casting its net far and wide, from high-pitched female vocals and an epic breakdown to dreamy, euphoric synthesizer melodies, the track was bound to appeal to a wider audience and cut a new path for trance music.

"Back in 1989, Lars and I discovered club music thanks to a weekly music program on Denmark's largest radio channel, P3, called Det DUR. They played all sorts of club music, ranging from techno and hip hop to dance and soul. We soon found out that it was the electronic material we had a love for.

Before we knew it, we were listening to bands such as Nitzer Ebb and Front 242—those that pushed a more heavy, industrial sound. These acts set the basis for the hardcore techno sound we went for when we eventually started producing ourselves.

"When we were about sixteen years old and still lived at our parents' place, we bought our first piece of gear—an EMU Emax 2, one of the first so-called low-budget samplers back then. It came at a price that would equal four thousand Euro today and didn't even come with a hard drive. We had to hide the sampler at my house, so Lars's parents didn't discover that we had spent so much money on music equipment.

The sampler had a sixteen-track real-time sequencer, meaning it wasn't possible to quantise or copy anything when recorded in the sequencer. Also, we had two MB of RAM memory at our disposal, so we could only sample about twelve seconds of sound. After that, we bought various Roland tools, such as a Juno keyboard, a TR-909 drum machine and a TB-303 synthesizer."

The duo's first release as Zekt followed in 1992. "We managed to release several hardcore tracks through German label Adam & Eve under that name, while eventually taking our work into more experimental territories. One of our tracks, External, was even licensed for one of the infamous Thunderdome gabber compilations."

Being a driving force of the Danish underground scene, Frederiksen and Weile regularly performed live at techno parties throughout the country. "These performances were a logistic nightmare and went wrong several times. We once performed at one of the largest Danish festivals, which was broadcasted live on the national radio, during which the synchronisation between our drum machine, synthesizer and sequencer kept failing us. Hence, we had to start one of our tracks over again three times. Still, playing live made it absolutely worth it."

In 1999, the duo received a cassette of a recording

of a Judge Jules' radio show on BBC Radio One. "That tape brought us to tune in to his weekly show and got us hooked to the British club trance sound that he was pushing. We then started to produce club trance, with a dream of having a track played by Judge Jules on one of his shows.

Back then, Lars used to work at a large recording studio in Copenhagen, which had been in existence for many years already. They had a stockroom full with all their old recordings and there we found an ADAT tape comprising all separate tracks from a ten year old album of a well-known Danish singer. The tape featured a track that didn't make it to the album and had therefore never been released.

"We used those vocals during our next studio sessions, which resulted in Light A Rainbow a few months later. Next, we tracked down the songwriter and played the track for him, but he didn't like it and said that we couldn't use the vocals.

We were disappointed but nevertheless started to send demo CDs to a selection of British, Dutch and German labels, as most trance records came from these areas. One of the said labels, Drizzly, called us one evening to share their enthusiasm about the record. As we began to converse further, there happened to be a good chemistry and Drizzly offered us a record contract. And curiously enough, when informing the songwriter about this proposal he suddenly liked the track!

Soon after Drizzly released Light A Rainbow, the record was picked up by Jive/Zomba. "Zomba was ready to fork out a serious amount of money on a video plus remixes, but the Danish singer wasn't interested in being part of a video clip nor to perform the track live. So the label suggested we work with a model, who could pretend to be the singer."

Remixes from various artists followed soon after. Yet, the most expensive remix—courtesy of ATB—initially turned into a disappointment for the record company. "His remix turned out to be different from his usual sound and not that commercially appealing. That was, until that remix received airplay by Judge Jules on BBC Radio One and everything was fine again…

"The success of Light A Rainbow made it possible for us to start our own studio in Copenhagen, where Lars is still working these days. From there, we were able to create a string of other productions using different monikers, whilst setting up F&W Records. Our music became more hard and clubby. Also, another two Tukan singles landed but never reached the same level of attention. It was nevertheless an incredibly fun time and Light A Rainbow brings back loads of good memories to us."

YOJI BIOMEHANIKA
—*A Theme From Banginglobe* (2002)
Yoji Mabuchi, Japan

Ever since he made his debut in the world of DJing and electronic music production, the name of Yoji Mabuchi, alias Yoji Biomehanika, is impossible to dissociate from his fictional, rock star-like character's exuberant appearance and energetic performances. Mabuchi played a significant part in the birth and growth of the newly enforced hard trance movement around the turn of the millennium. With A Theme From Banginglobe, the Japanese producer pushed back the limits of the genre even further by merging tropes from styles as diverse as hard house, techno and trance in a single track.

"Music has played a particularly important part in my life since high school. I didn't like to hang out with crowds of people, so I spent a lot of time working on my music solo. I was mainly influenced by genres like progressive rock, punk and new wave, so I picked up an acoustic guitar but soon moved to play electric guitar as I really loved the sound of distortion and flanger."

By the time Machubi finished high school, he started playing the bass guitar in what would become one of Japan's best-known punk-rock bands, Laughin' Nose. "The band revolutionised the history of Japanese music. In the early nineties, however, I took an interest in electronic dance music. I discovered some records from German trance labels at a local record shop, which had a big influence on me as a producer.

I felt I could be more creative in producing dance music than with rock music. The first equipment that I obtained included a Roland Juno-106 synthesizer, a MC-500 sequencer and a TR-606 drum machine. All the different influences from my youth came together in my sound, being uplifting and melodic yet with a hard edge."

As Mabuchi further developed his unique musical identity, it didn't take long for his catalogue to flesh out. His sound was radically different from the European records that came out at that time. "When I had my first tracks ready, I sent demo tapes to a couple of German record labels and received great responses from both Dos Or Die and No Respect.

As Dos Or Die was the first to make a move, Rendezvous De Telepathie was released on that label in 1994, which became my first international release and opened many doors for me. A couple of years later, I decided to start my own label Hellhouse. Interesting to note is that I based the label in the United Kingdom, as there were no proper Japanese distributors available for my kind of sound."

Following on from a string of releases on Hellhouse, Machubi's 2002-released A Theme From Banginglobe went on to play a key role in bridging the gap between the harder styles and trance music on a global scale. "Banginglobe was the name of a festival stage that was part of AVEX Trance in 2002. AVEX was, and still is, one of the leading music companies in Japan. The event took place only once and I was, invited to make the theme song for that particular stage.

> "A Theme From Banginglobe brings back special memories to me, as it marks the first time hard dance became visible on such a large scale in Japan."

"The track itself was produced in a very short time. I had the melody in my head and it took me little time to record it with my Virus Access synthesizer at the Hellhouse studio in Osaka. That same year, Ferry Corsten was on tour in Japan and we happened to play a club gig together. He listened to my set that night, which included A Theme From Banginglobe. The riff in the middle caught Ferry's attention straight away. Someone working for the record department of AVEX told him it was a track of mine, which would be released on Hellhouse."

The next time Corsten paid a visit, the two had dinner in Mabuchi's hometown of Osaka. "Ferry wanted to make a System F remix of A Theme From Banginglobe, as the original version was too hard for him to play in his sets. Alternatively, I agreed on making a remix of Gouryella's track Ligaya.

"When the record came out on Hellhouse, the sales were initially not really good. Without any promotional efforts, we sold about five thousand copies—which was quite limited compared to other releases on the label. However, many influential artists played it and Ferry's remix definitely helped to make the track known to a wider audience.

As I was initially only booked for hard-house related events, I became more connected to the hard dance, trance and techno scenes. My sound became more multi-functional and allowed me to play more larger-sized gigs across Europe, such as Trance Energy in the Netherlands.

"I cannot compare my sound to any other music and I never thought of copying any other artists in the process—I just follow my heart. A Theme From Banginglobe brings back special memories to me, as it marks the first time hard dance became visible on such a large scale in Japan."

YORK—*The Awakening* (1997)
Torsten Stenzel, Germany

Formed by brothers Torsten and Jörg Stenzel, German act York saw the light of day in 1997. Whereas Jörg found himself mostly drawn to stringed instruments, Torsten's first introduction to music came when he began piano lessons at the age of five. Joining forces as York, the Stenzel brothers subsequently laid the foundation to a solar-powered, Balearic-infused body of work, of which The Awakening undeniably remains the keystone.

"Classical music and music theory played a key role in our youth. My first major influences, however, were Pink Floyd, Kraftwerk, Front 242 and also some songs by Mike Oldfield. These acts fuelled my interest in electronic music and I became particularly fascinated with synthesizers. So, with the money I received from my family for my communion, I bought my first piece of equipment, a Yamaha DX 100. I was around fourteen years old. At that time I switched to playing the church organ and graduated as an organist at the age of seventeen, then playing the one in our hometown for two years."

Torsten's musical orientation took another turn in the early nineties when he discovered the then-growing house and techno movement. "When I started working on DJ Taucher's album Return To Atlantis, we invited my brother Jörg to play some guitar on the chill-out tracks (as I still loved guitars, especially in this Pink Floyd-like atmosphere). The success of the album made me decide to explore options outside of Germany, so I built a recording studio in Ibiza. After setting this up, I promptly started working on various projects again, including York."

By then, Jörg had become an outstanding contributor in the studio. While working on ideas to combine guitar riffs with current house and trance grooves, Torsten joined in and York was born. "When working on The Awakening in 1997, we simply tried that same recipe again: Jörg played this amazing guitar melody, which ended up being the main hook of the song."

> "We created our world just for the music and the lifestyle and didn't even know that our early tracks were considered trance."

The Awakening was initially released on Stenzel's own label Planetlove Records under the name of Big Brother Is Watching You. "Andreas Tomalla, aka Talla 2XLC—the owner of Suck Me Plasma, played the track over and over again and wanted to reissue it on his label. Talla didn't like the name so we changed the title to The Awakening and released it via Suck Me Plasma, because his distribution was way better organised than mine. The Awakening made its way without any major promotion and yet it sold over two hundred fifty thousand copies.

"We created our world just for the music and the lifestyle and didn't even know that our early tracks were considered trance. We could test everything straight away in clubs such as Music Hall and Dorian Gray in Frankfurt to get a taste of the crowds' reaction. That vibe was just amazing and a new era arose with all these synthesizers and possibilities.

Apart from that, we partied incredibly hard. Money wasn't important at all and I think that's the biggest difference with today's scene. Although my brother was only partially involved with the York project, we still maintain a good relationship. The music was just a hobby to him and after making it big in the music world he just returned to his 'normal' life, while I continued working in this industry."

DJ Jean at Sensation, 2001 © ID&T

LABELS

Record labels are trademarks associated with the production, manufacturing, distribution, marketing promotion and publishing of music, while conducting talent scouting and developing artist's careers. The term 'record label' derives from the circular label in the center of a vinyl record which prominently displays the manufacturer's name, along with other key information.

As major labels only began to show an interest in electronic music in more recent times, independent record labels played a crucial role in the development of trance music. These institutions directed the genre towards specific shifts and turns, generating further business opportunities. Concepts were developed at times when new media sources such as the internet played a limited role, or no role at all, in creating brand visibility. Meanwhile, other critical factors made their businesses flourish at both a local and an international level.

The personal involvement of label managers has been equally important in the development of both artists and releases, as their record labels evolved into comprehensive and widespread high-quality platforms. Many attempted to publish ground-breaking trance records over time, yet only a handful were able to turn their vision into a long-running and profitable business model.

In this section, seventy-five platforms are highlighted that contributed to the development of the genre in their own right. Low-profile, personal projects rub shoulders with highly visible, globally successful ventures. Some have been around for only a brief period of time, others withstood the test of time and are still active today. Some of these labels were first-movers, releasing only a handful of groundbreaking records, while other labels jumped on the latest trends and landed commercially viable releases right away. This market balance between creativity, passion and commercial appeal were essential in order to push a genre forward.

Additionally, five influential label managers reflect on their business ventures. These stories provide an answer to the way label managers balanced positioning a strong brand at a time when globalisation and technological innovations, but also expanded artistic endeavours and economic feasibility, came together. Proving the breadth of their vision and long-term relevancy, all interviewees are still active in today's music industry.

The country tag refers to the country of origin of the label. If a year is mentioned within brackets, this indicates the year of closing. Only five notable label-related artists are mentioned under the notable artists tag.

A

A TRANCE COMMUNICATION RELEASE
Country: United Kingdom
Founded by: Tim Stark
Founded in: 1998 (- 2005)
Notable art.: Free Radical
Geoff Lawz Project
Insigma
Pulser
Rapid Eye

ABFAHRT RECORDS
Country: Germany
Founded by: Torsten Fenslau
Founded in: 1989 (- 1993)
Notable art.: Culture Beat
In-Trance
Kim Sanders
Near Dark
Out Of The Ordinary

ADDITIVE
Country: United Kingdom
Founded in: 1996 (- 2004)
Notable art.: Ayla
DJ Remy
Filterheadz
Solid Sessions
Velvet Girl
X-Cabs

ALPHABET CITY
Country: Germany
Founded by: Klaus Derichs
Marc Romboy
Founded in: 1992 (- 2014)
Notable art.: Caucasuss
Future Breeze
Emmanuel Top
Marc et Claude
Microwave Prince

ANJUNABEATS
Country: United Kingdom
Founded by: Jono Grant
Paavo Siljamäki
Tony McGuinness
Founded in: 2000
Notable art.: Above & Beyond
Aspekt
OceanLab
P.O.S.
Tranquility Base

ANTLER-SUBWAY
Country: Belgium
Founded by: Maurice Engelen
Roland Beelen
Founded in: 1989 (- 2006)
Notable art.: 2 Fabiola
Cold Sensation
Emmanuel Top
Lords Of Acid
Milk Incorporated

ARMADA MUSIC
Country: Netherlands
Founded by: Armin van Buuren
David Lewis
Maykel Piron
Founded in: 2003
Notable art.: Armin van Buuren
Filo & Peri
Mark Otten
Markus Schulz
M.I.K.E.

AZWAN TRANSMISSIONS
Country: Australia
Founded by: Richie McNeill
Founded in: 1993 (- 1998)
Notable art.: Dimension
Sonic Animation
Spiritualist
Stormboy
Viridian

B

BEDROCK RECORDS
Country: United Kingdom
Founded by: John Digweed
Nick Muir
Founded in: 1999
Notable art.: Bedrock
Guy J
John Digweed
Pole Folder
Steve Lawler

BLACK HOLE RECORDINGS
Country: Netherlands
Founded by: Arny Bink
Tijs Verwest
Founded in: 1997
Notable art.: Andain
DJ Montana
DJ Tiësto
Midway
Yahel

BLUE MOON RELEASED
Country: United Kingdom
Founded by: Simon Ghahary
Founded in: 1995 (- 2005)
Notable art.: Cydonia
Etnica
Juno Reactor
Total Eclipse
X-Dream

BONZAI RECORDS
Country: Belgium
Founded by: Christian Pieters
Frank Sels
Yves Deruyter
Founded in: 1992
Notable art.: Airwave
Da Hool
Jones & Stephenson
Push
Yves Deruyter

BORDER COMMUNITY
- Country: United Kingdom
- Founded by: James Holden
- Founded in: 2003
- Notable art.: Avus
  - Fairmont
  - Nathan Fake
  - Petter
  - The MFA

C

CYBER RECORDS
- Country: Netherlands
- Founded by: Johan Groenewegen
- Founded in: 1994 (- 2009)
- Notable art.: Armin
  - Argonout
  - Continuous Cool
  - Yahel
  - World Tour

D

DATA RECORDS
- Country: United Kingdom
- Founded by: James Palumbo
- Founded in: 1999 (- 2010)
- Notable art.: iiO
  - Kamaya Painters
  - Lost Witness
  - Rising Star
  - Schiller

DBX RECORDS
- Country: Italy
- Founded by: Giuseppe Troccoli
- Founded in: 1993 (- 2008)
- Notable art.: D.A.T.A.
  - Daniele Gas
  - DJ Miki
  - Nylon Moon
  - Robert Miles

DECONSTRUCTION
- Country: United Kingdom
- Founded by: Keith Blackhurst
  - Pete Hadfield
- Founded in: 1986
- Notable art.: Deep Dish
  - Robert Miles
  - Sasha
  - Spiritualized
  - Way Out West

DELIRIUM
- Country: Germany
- Founded by: Jörg Henze
- Founded in: 1992 (- 1998)
- Notable art.: Atom Heart
  - Nihilist
  - Psilocybin
  - Redeye
  - Solar Eclipse

DEVIANT RECORDS
- Country: United Kingdom
- Founded by: Rob Deacon
- Founded in: 1994 (- 2007)
- Notable art.: Node
  - Paul van Dyk
  - Pentatonik
  - Schematix
  - Witchman

DRAGONFLY RECORDS
- Country: United Kingdom
- Founded by: Martin Glover
- Founded in: 1993 (- 2003)
- Notable art.: Doof
  - Hallucinogen
  - Heather Nova
  - Man With No Name
  - Shakta

E

EVE RECORDS
- Country: United Kingdom
- Founded by: Simon Eve
- Founded in: 1995 (- 2014)
- Notable art.: David Craig
  - Halogen
  - Markus Schulz
  - Paplo Gargano
  - Steve Gibbs

EXPERIMENTAL
- Country: United States
- Founded by: Silvio Tancredi
- Founded in: 1991 (- 1995)
- Notable art.: Aurasfere
  - Bio Dreams
  - Diffusion
  - Symphony Of Love
  - The Rising Sons

EYE Q MUSIC
- Country: Germany
- Founded by: Heinz Roth
  - Matthias Hoffmann,
  - Sven Väth
- Founded in: 1990 (- 1998)
- Notable art.: Sven Väth
  - Cygnus X
  - Earth Nation
  - Hardfloor
  - Zyon

F

F COMMUNICATIONS
- Country: France
- Founded by: Eric Morand
  - Laurent Garnier
- Founded in: 1994 (- 2008)
- Notable art.: Aqua Bassino
  - Laurent Garnier
  - Nova Nova
  - Scan X
  - St Germain

FAX +49-69/450464

Country	Germany
Founded by	Peter Kuhlmann
Founded in	1992 (- 2012)
Notable art.	4 Voice
	Move D
	Pete Namlook
	Testu Inoue
	The Dark Side Of The Moog

FRANKFURT BEAT PRODUCTIONS

Country	Germany
Founded by	Jens Maspfuhl
	Mario De Bellis
	Ralf Zintel
Founded in	1993 (- 2000)
Notable art.	Circuit
	Paragon
	Robotnico
	Syncrotron
	Tronic

FULL FREQUENCY RANGE RECORDINGS

Country	United Kingdom
Founded by	Pete Tong
	Phil Howells
Founded in	1986
Notable art.	Lil Louis
	Nalin & Kane
	Orbital
	Salt 'N' Pepa
	Satoshi Tomiie

FUNDAMENTAL RECORDINGS

Country	Netherlands
Founded by	Raz Nitzan
Founded in	2002 (- 2007)
Notable art.	A Situation
	Electrovoya
	Progression
	Solid Globe
	Yahel

G

GAIA TONTRÄGER

Country	Germany
Founded by	Andreas Roll
Founded in	1991 (- 2001)
Notable art.	Dharma 7
	Evolution
	Mandra Gora
	S.M.I.L.E.
	X-Tron

GANG GO MUSIC

Country	Germany
Founded by	Gottfried Engels
	Louis Spillmann
Founded in	1997 (- 2005)
Notable art.	Blank & Jones
	Fragma
	Paffendorf
	Perpetuous Dreamer
	Talla2XLC

GUERILLA RECORDS

Country	United Kingdom
Founded by	William Wainwright
	Disc O'Dell
Founded in	1990 (- 2003)
Notable art.	React 2 Rhythm
	Spank Spank
	Spooky
	Trance Induction
	William Orbit

H

HOOJ CHOONS

Country	United Kingdom
Founded by	Jeremy Dickens
	Phil Howells
Founded in	1991 (- 2003)
Notable art.	Accadia
	Energy 52
	Lost Tribe
	Miro
	Solarstone

HOOK RECORDINGS

Country	Scotland
Founded by	Chris Cowie
Founded in	1993 (- 2010)
Notable art.	Canyon
	De Niro
	Third Man
	Transa
	X-Cabs

I

ID&T

Country	Netherlands
Founded by	Duncan Stutterheim
	Irfan van Ewijk
	Theo Lelie
Founded in	1992 (- 2005)
Notable art.	Human Evolution
	Marco V
	Rank 1
	Robert Gitelman
	Svenson & Gielen

IMPORTANT RECORDS

Country	Germany
Founded by	Udo Welcker
Founded in	1993 (- 2012)
Notable art.	Acrid Abeyance
	Moguai
	Liquid Bass
	Paranoia X
	Pergon

IST RECORDS

Country	United States
Founded by	Leonardo Didesiderio
Founded in	1993
Notable art.	Cyberia
	Laura Grabb
	Manga Corps
	Somatic Responses
	Zenith

J

LABELS

JOOF RECORDINGS
- Country: United Kingdom
- Founded by: John Fleming
- Founded in: 1999
- Notable art.: AR52
  - Astral Projection
  - Fusion
  - The Digital Blonde
  - Ultrasonic

K

KOMPAKT SCHALLPLATTEN
- Country: Germany
- Founded by: Jörg Burger
  - Jürgen Paape
  - Michael Mayer
  - Reinhard Voigt
  - Wolfgang Voigt
- Founded in: 1998
- Notable art.: Dettinger
  - GAS
  - Kaito
  - Superpitcher
  - Thomas Fehlmann

KONTOR RECORDS
- Country: Germany
- Founded by: Jens Thele
- Founded in: 1996
- Notable art.: ATB
  - Blank & Jones
  - Scooter
  - Sunbeam
  - Woody van Eyden

L

LOW SPIRIT RECORDINGS
- Country: Germany
- Founded by: Fabian Lenz
  - Klaus Jankuhn
  - Maximilian Lenz
  - Sandra Molzahn
  - William Röttger
- Founded in: 1986 (- 2009)
- Notable art.: K-Paul
  - RMB
  - Suspicious
  - Three 'N One
  - Westbam

LUSH RECORDINGS
- Country: United Kingdom
- Founded by: Laurence Potter
  - Paul Marlow
- Founded in: 1994 (- 1998)
- Notable art.: The South Of Trance
  - Friends Lovers & Family
  - Mr. Oz & Larry Lush
  - The Faith Foundation
  - WLR

M

MANIFESTO RECORDS
- Country: United Kingdom
- Founded by: Ben Cherrill
  - Eddie Gordon
  - Judge Jules
  - Luke Neville
- Founded in: 1995 (- 2006)
- Notable art.: Junkie XL
  - The Space Brothers
  - Todd Terry
  - Yomanda
  - York

MASSIVE DRIVE
- Country: Netherlands
- Founded by: Mark van Dale
- Founded in: 1997 (- 2011)
- Notable art.: DJ Ton T.B.
  - Erik de Koning
  - Lost Lynx
  - Rainbox
  - Three Drives On A Vinyl

MASTERMINDED FOR SUCCESS
- Country: Germany
- Founded by: Mark Reeder
- Founded in: 1990 (- 2007)
- Notable art.: Alien Nation
  - Cosmic Baby
  - Humate
  - Microglobe
  - Paul van Dyk

MATSURI PRODUCTIONS
- Country: United Kingdom
- Founded by: John Perloff
  - Tsuyoshi Suzuki
- Founded in: 1994 (- 1999)
- Notable art.: Astral Projection
  - Koxbox
  - Joujouka
  - Prana
  - Sandman

MEDIA RECORDS
- Country: Italy
- Founded by: Gianfranco Bortolotti
- Founded in: 1986
- Notable art.: Gigi D'Agostino
  - Joy Kitikonti
  - Mario Più
  - Mauro Picotto
  - Saccoman

MOSTIKO
- Country: Belgium
- Founded in: 2000
- Notable art.: DJ Gert
  - Junkie XL
  - Minimalistix
  - Orion Too
  - Parla & Pardoux

N

NEO
- Country: United Kingdom
- Founded by: Eddie Gordon
- Founded in: 1998 (- 2002)

Notable art.
- Darude
- Inflexion
- Liquid Child
- Rocco & Heist
- The Thrillseekers

NETTWERK
Country: Canada
Founded by: Dan Fraser, Mark Jowett, Ric Arboit, Terry McBride
Founded in: 1984
Notable art.:
- Conjure One
- Delerium
- Dido
- Sarah McLachlan
- Skinny Puppy

NO RESPECT RECORDS
Country: Germany
Founded by: Ramon Zenker, Jens Lissat
Founded in: 1991 (- 2000)
Notable art.:
- Aqualoop
- Exit 'EEE'
- Hardfloor
- Mindspace
- Phenomania

NOOM RECORDS
Country: Germany
Founded by: Joachim Keil
Founded in: 1993 (- 2003)
Notable art.:
- Commander Tom
- Jim Clarke
- Nuclear Hyde
- Toronto
- Twisted

P

PERFECTO RECORDS
Country: United Kingdom
Founded by: Paul Oakenfold
Founded in: 1989
Notable art.:
- BT
- Grace
- Jan Johnston
- Paul Oakenfold
- Timo Maas

PLANET DOG
Country: United Kingdom
Founded by: Michael Dog, Bob Dog
Founded in: 1993 (- 1998)
Notable art.:
- Banco De Gaia
- Children Of The Bong
- Eat Static
- Future Loop Foundation
- Timeshard

PLANETARY CONSCIOUSNESS
Country: Germany
Founded by: Hardy Heller
Founded in: 1998 (- 2003)

Notable art.
- AMbassador
- DJ Tiësto
- Dominion
- Gouryella
- H.H.

PLATIPUS
Country: United Kingdom
Founded by: Simon Berry
Founded in: 1993 (- 2010)
Notable art.:
- Albion
- Art Of Trance
- Robert Miles
- Libra
- Union Jack

POD COMMUNICATION
Country: Germany
Founded by: Olaf Finkbeiner
Founded in: 1992 (- 1996)
Notable art.:
- Atom Heart
- Blissed
- Detune
- Ongaku
- Sideral

POSITIVA RECORDS
Country: United Kingdom
Founded by: Nick Halkes
Founded in: 1993 (- 2010)
Notable art.:
- B.B.E.
- Binary Finary
- DJ Quicksilver
- Reflekt
- Storm

R

REACT
Country: United Kingdom
Founded by: Thomas Foley, James Horrocks
Founded in: 1991 (- 2017)
Notable art.:
- Age Of Love
- Blu Peter
- Elevator
- GTO
- The Source

RISING HIGH RECORDS
Country: United Kingdom
Founded by: Casper Pound
Founded in: 1991 (- 2003)
Notable art.:
- Air Liquide
- Cybordelics
- Legend B
- The Hypnotist
- Paragliders

R&S RECORDS
Country: Belgium
Founded by: Renaat Vandepapeliere, Sabine Maes
Founded in: 1984
Notable art.:
- Aphex Twin
- CJ Bolland
- Jam & Spoon

Joey Beltram
Westbam

S

SILVER PLANET RECORDINGS
Country United Kingdom
Founded by David Conway
Founded in 1995 (- 2009)
Notable art. Chris Salt
James Holden
Marco Zaffarano
Sadie Glutz
Timo Maas

SPINNIN' RECORDS
Country Netherlands
Founded by Eelco van Kooten
Roger de Graaf
Founded in 1999
Notable art. 4 Strings
Driftwood
Randy Katana
Sander van Doorn
The Mystery

SPIRIT ZONE RECORDINGS
Country Germany
Founded by Wolfgang Matthias Ahrens
Founded in 1994 (- 2005)
Notable art. Electric Universe
Patchwork
Shiva Chandra
Space Tribe
S.U.N. Project

SUBWAY RECORDS
Country Italy
Founded by Claudio Diva
Founded in 1994 (- 2008)
Notable art. Daniele Maffei
DJ Dado
Gigi D'Agostino
Lello B.
Tout Paris

SUCK ME PLASMA
Country Germany
Founded by Andreas Tomalla
Founded in 1989 (- 2001)
Notable art. Aqualite
Dance 2 Trance
Final Fantasy
Sunbeam
Tranceformer

SUPERSTITION
Country Germany
Founded by Marc Chung
Tobias Lampe
Founded in 1993 (- 2003)
Notable art. Humate
Jens
L.S.G.
Marmion
Mijk van Dijk

T

TASTE RECORDINGS
Country Netherlands
Founded by Remy Unger
Founded in 1994 (- 2004)
Notable art. DJ Remy
Gregor
Outline
Roland Klinkenberg
The Wavecatcher

TRANS'PACT PRODUCTIONS
Country France
Founded by Barbara Marillier
Gilbert Thévenet
Founded in 1992 (- 1997)
Notable art. Asia 2001
Progressive transe
Section X
Subliminal
Transvase

TRIGGER
Country Germany
Founded in 1992 (- 1996)
Notable art. Confusion A
Energy Flash
E-Reaction
Padre Terra
S.M.I.L.E.

TSUNAMI
Country Netherlands
Founded by Ferry Corsten
Robert Smit
Founded in 1997 (- 2007)
Notable art. Gouryella
System F
Kid Vicious
Matt Darey
Ronald van Gelderen

V

VANDIT RECORDS
Country Germany
Founded by Matthias Paul
Founded in 1999
Notable art. Jose Amnesia
NU NRG
Paul van Dyk
Second Sun
The Thrillseekers

VENOM RECORDINGS
Country Germany
Founded by Andreas Schmidt
Founded in 2002 (- 2007)
Notable art. Ace Da Brain
Airfire
Andreas Schmidt
Bacedl
Talla 2XLC

X

XTRAVAGANZA RECORDINGS

Country	United Kingdom
Founded by	Alex Gold
Founded in	1996 (- 2015)
Notable art.	Agnelli & Nelson
	Airscape
	Armin van Buuren
	Chicane
	Three Drives On A Vinyl

Y

YETI RECORDS

Country	Belgium
Founded by	Hessel Tieter
	Lieven van den Broeck
Founded in	1995 (- 2006)
Notable art.	Delerium
	Green Velvet
	Lost Witness
	Mr. Sam
	Red Screen

#

23RD PRECINCT RECORDINGS LTD

Country	Scotland
Founded by	Billy Kiltie
Founded in	1991 (- 2013)
Notable art.	Distant Drums
	Fade
	Gypsy
	Havana
	Mukkaa

Marco V at Innercity, 2003 © Rutger Geerling/ID&T

BLACK HOLE RECORDINGS
Arny Bink
15 March 1970, Etten-Leur, Netherlands

"As a student I always found myself occupied with music, so I was lucky to land a side-job at Tunesville—the only record store in Breda that took care of import 12" vinyls. The owner also happened to run a record label and a record store in Rotterdam called Basic Beat, where Tijs Verwest worked behind the counter.

Back then, hardcore and gabber music gained momentum in the Netherlands and we noticed that compilation CDs were selling extremely well. Many artists and events launched their own series, yet a popular event named Hellraiser didn't release anything alike. So we created these unofficial, themed mix CDs called The Night Of The Hellraisers and each compilation easily sold about ten thousand copies.

Around that time, we went out at Belgian clubs such as Illusion and Club X, which got us into this harder trance sound that was brought by Bonzai. These experiences formed the basis for the Forbidden Paradise compilations, an idea I had contemplated for some time before they actually came out. The first two CDs were compilations crafted by me: after that, Tijs took care of the mixes. It was initially hard to find the music, because trance as such didn't exist to us and we were basically still shaping the sound.

In 1997, after about five years of working for Basic

Beat, the timing was ideal to do the same thing but for ourselves. I was fired from my job at Basic Beat because I started my own record label outside the company. Tijs had already left, so we had our hands free to start something on our own. There was this major gap in the market, as there were hardly any trance-oriented labels around. So it was easy for us to find a distributor and get started. It was also right before trance really took off in the Netherlands, as well as abroad.

That same year, Black Hole was born and we basically just continued what we did before: Tijs was really good at mixing CDs and I was handling the production and artwork. We started with the Magik 1 compilation, which sold well enough to fund our next projects. From then on, we grew organically and Tijs' Magik and In Search Of Sunrise mix series became our flagships to a more mainstream audience. Also, working with new artists was an organic process: they knew what we were doing and were eager to work with us.

The self-titled Black Hole label became a platform for the more melodic, emotion-driven music that Tijs selected. Yet, we also received a lot of music that didn't really fit that sound, but was really good as well. So we started categorising and created new labels for different sounds. In Trance We Trust was the first (and most successful) sublabel, emphasising more uptempo and uplifting club sounds.

Tijs launched his Magik Muzik sublabel, initially

covering his own music but which began incorporating other artists later on. Apart from that, we also set up various other, mostly short-lived, sublabels that operated in genres such as house and techno, including Black Hole Avanti and Wildlife. Still, some of the best-selling items were Tiësto's own works, most notably his albums Just Be and Elements Of Life as well as his In Concert DVDs—each of which sold about four hundred thousand copies worldwide.

As there wasn't any record store in Breda that specialised in electronic music, we filled that gap in 1998, right after we started the record label. We had the experience of running a shop at Basic Beat and Tunesville, so basically we just filled the racks of our own store with music we found and got started. Tijs signed new music and ran the store with friends like Montana and Dazzle, while I ran the label. It was that simple.

We offered mostly house, techno and trance. Our customers were from within the region, but also from Belgium. Magik attracted a lot of DJs who used to spend their budget from playing at bars and clubs on new records on a weekly basis. At some point, the store also became a point of interest for Tiësto fans from all over Europe.

We had some amazing moments within the first couple years of the new millennium. The label was successful in both musical and financial terms, the store became a solid meeting point for our friends and artists, while Tijs turned into this main icon of trance on an international level. The Black Hole imprint was in that sense a tool to bring him there, yet many other factors played a similarly important role.

Yet, Tijs left the company in 2009 because he didn't want to feel the pressure of running a record label and the responsibilities that go with it anymore. I expected his departure to have a major impact on us in various aspects. He was the label's main artist and his marketing boosted our platform in many ways.

Interestingly, other artists felt more empowered when Tijs left, as Black Hole was strongly built around Tiësto before. All the artists we worked with, such as Andain, BT, Cosmic Gate, JES and Zoo Brazil, stayed with Black Hole and seized the opportunity to play an increasingly important role. There seemed to be more balance within the label.

> "Tijs signed new music and ran the store with friends like Montana and Dazzle, while I ran the label. It was that simple."

The market change from vinyl to digital had a major influence on our existence. Instead of being able to sell a serious amount of records with major turnovers, the digital market meant very low profit margins. There is no market control and the market becomes overloaded with average music. Also, illegal downloads of pretty much all releases are widely available.

Ultimately, the digitalisation of the market made us decide to close the Magik store in 2006. Sales rapidly decreased in the early noughties: at one point we looked at our store profits and noticed we only made about ten thousand Euro in an entire year. Unfortunately, there seemed to be little to no future for a physical vinyl store.

On the other hand, the internet has offered the music industry many new ways to connect to their audience. I love the fact that an MP3 or WAV file is never out of stock and that web stores such as Amazon have almost everything ready to order. Also, social media offers fans the opportunity to connect directly with artists and labels.

Trance defined our identity as Black Hole in the early years and we still focus mostly on trance music these days. The genre as a whole has evolved over time: the production standards have matured, but I also think that the width of the genre—in terms of sound—has been more clearly defined. For the core fans, the genre was never gone and we have only developed correspondingly to its overall development."

Arny's favourite Black Hole tracks:
ANDAIN—*Beautiful Things*
BT—*Mercury & Solace*
DJ TIËSTO—*Flight 643*

BONZAI RECORDS
Christian Pieters
30 December 1965, Antwerp, Belgium

"Bonzai Records was born in 1992 in the back of a DJ shop called Blitz, in Antwerp. Many of my regular customers—including CJ Bolland, DJ Bountyhunter and Yves Deruyter—were into producing music, so the idea to get a studio up and running was thrown around.

Soon after, the studios were set up. Word spread quickly and the Bonzai label was founded. The studios were occupied day and night and after a short period we had a number of releases that really put Bonzai on the map. In those first years, many other talented producers joined our ranks, including Airwave, Dave Davis, DJ Fire, DJ Ghost, Gregory Dewindt, Insider, Marino Stephano, M.I.K.E., Phi Phi and Philippe Van Mullem.

Back then we didn't worry too much about genres and just released music with 'fun' in mind: fun for those who made the music and fun for our rapidly expanding fan base. In the early nineties there wasn't much trance around to begin with, but tracks like The Age Of Love were making headway. It soon became clear to me that trance was gonna be the next big thing alongside house and techno.

In 1994, around the time when the progressive trance sound really kicked in, I held a residency together with Phi Phi at Extreme—a club that had just opened its doors in Affligem. One of Phi Phi's tracks, Eternally (under the Quadran moniker), became the trigger that gave birth to the Bonzai Trance Progressive label. I really loved that sound, which obviously resulted in the many trance releases we subsequently published.

Our studio complex—the 'cockpit'—expanded into three studios. More than ninety per cent of our releases were produced here. Our offices were on the first floor, which resulted in me being either in the shop or one of the studios. Everyone who worked there knew very well what kind of sound I expected for the label: I also pushed them in that direction. There was a cool kind of magic going on between everyone: a camaraderie between artists, advising and helping each other, which eventually led to some of the biggest tunes being released at that time.

The first record we released was E-Mission by Stockhousen in 1992, made by the now-deceased Liza 'N' Eliaz. Elisa was a transvestite with long, grey hair. She wore a bright pink coat and weird glasses. We thought it wouldn't hurt that our first release came from her hand: she was the musical translation of who we wanted to be. Yet, the record didn't appeal at all. Release numbers three, four and five on the original Bonzai Records imprint—Animals by Yves Deruyter, Bountyhunter by DJ Bountyhunter and Reality by Phrenetic System, respectively—eventually opened many doors for the label and its artists.
As the DJ shop gained more popularity, our studios

were continuously occupied, licensing requests came in and bookings were over the top, with some of us having weekends filled with eight to ten gigs. I figured we might as well promote the label with some t-shirts for our artists, which inadvertently created a massive hype for Bonzai merchandise amongst clubbers. Over seven hundred thousand Bonzai t-shirts and bomber jackets were sold. I guess I never really felt the success coming, since none of us actually thought about such things.

One of these unforgettable moments was when we first heard a new demo from Mike Dierickx in our office. He had prepared two songs in the Bonzai studio and proudly presented them to us. We first listened to Prisma: a really good track, but the track that caught the light was its B-side. Halfway in, everyone in the office was dancing on top of their desk. Mike was shocked, he had no idea what was happening. We told him that this track will be his breakthrough. And so it happened: Universal Nation by Push turned into one of the greatest Belgian dance classics, if you ask me. Only Mike thought differently at the time.

With the end of the nineties came the trend of downloading music illegally. We noticed how our incomes were gradually crumbling. Moreover, just at that moment an important deal with Sony fell through. We wanted to gain a foothold in Wallonia and France and therefore made a compilation CD entitled Boum, with a lot of banging songs. But the Twin Tower attack happened right ahead of the big promotional campaign. Sony suddenly no longer wanted to promote CDs with the name Boum.

We had to bear all our losses, which engaged the decline of the label. Regardless of this financial situation, Lightning Records—the parent company of Bonzai Records—was just building a new office. When a bank became interested in buying up half of the site, it could have saved the company—but we refused. Luckily, shortly after our bankruptcy the company was able to make a new start.

After a few difficult years, we were able to regain our place in the industry by immediately focusing our attention on the digital market. And so our company gradually started to grow again. Our main output medium during the nineties was vinyl: the vinyl industry is a costly business, but in the early nineties it was the best way to reach all dance music minded people. The market was packed with vinyl stores—I think Belgium alone had close to one hundred specialist stores. But today, most of them are gone, including the big dance music vinyl distributors.

Distribution and vinyl stores were the primary filters to strain the flow of incoming releases, ultimately feeding the client with their exact demands. Nowadays anyone can start a digital label, which is visible in the state of today's market. And there's really no one out there that can go through the twenty five thousand new tracks being uploaded every week on Beatport alone. So a lot of stuff remains unheard, not well promoted enough and simply vanishes into anonymity.

Maybe we had a bit of luck with the new beat scene at the end of the eighties: the whole world had its eyes glued to Belgium and out of that movement the first house and techno labels such as R&S Records were born and then we followed shortly after.

It's about having the right 'momentum' in the market: it's a truckload of factors that need to match up at the same time. I guess we were in the right place, with the right posse, with the right genre at the right moment in time. The critical elements are always the same, the label needs to put out hits. And in the nineties, hits were made in clubs. We had resident DJs in almost all the top clubs and venues, so it was easy to promote our tunes. It's a bit like the main stage festival DJs of today: they butter up each other until it bleeds, nothing new there. That's how it goes now and that's how it went down in the past as well.

In all honesty, what one calls trance today is not my thing anymore. I started struggling with the genre back in 2002 or 2003, which became noticeable in the releases we put out in the following years. Around 2006, it became clear to me and my associate that we needed a big change to actually enjoy ourselves again, which was—and still is—working in the music business and running labels.

Today, our trance department is handled by label

managers and represents just a very small part of the genres we put out. So yes, trance has influenced Bonzai twice: once in the early nineties at the start of the trance boom, and later on when we couldn't identify ourselves with the genre anymore."

Christian's favourite Bonzai tracks:
CHERRY MOON TRAX—*The House Of House*
JONES & STEPHENSON—*The First Rebirth*
PUSH—*Universal Nation*

F COMMUNICATIONS
Eric Morand
26 December 1964, Marseille, France

"My first introduction into the music industry came with working at a public radio—as a DJ and music programmer—before landing a job in public relations at Scorpio Music in Paris. In 1988, about one year and a half later, I moved on to become label manager at Polygram. We handled various electronic music labels from abroad for the French market, such as FFFR—the British powerhouse label of Pete Tong back then.

By the late eighties, Fnac—a company that was running a chain of record stores in France since the seventies—wanted to launch an electronic music subsidiary, called Fnac Music Dance Division. They knew me from my work at Polygram and asked me to set up the label and take care of A&R in 1991.
   It was a little earlier—in 1989 or 1990, at one of the very first raves in France—that I met Laurent Garnier. I had heard about him for the first time about a year earlier, at a venue called The Palace in Paris, and also read interviews of his in various magazines. As I was still working at Polygram, I used to regularly provide him with the latest FFFR promos.

Soon after, I would join Laurent on his tours across the country, jumping into his car with some friends to drive to his gigs. Back then, I already had the idea to sign more French artists on Fnac. Seeing the talent and passion of Laurent, he was the first I signed in 1991. Yet, French labels pushing French artists were pretty much unheard of back then. Also, there wasn't a proper infrastructure in place to run an electronic music label.

Mastering, for example, was impossible: all engineers were trained to work on hip-hop, rock or French music, not techno. We faced a similar problem with pressing records, as there were only two pressing plants available. There was also a lack of proper distribution channels, as the French ones were exclusively focused on importing music from abroad. Those were major challenges for us and it took a solid two years to develop these networks.

By early 1993, we finally started to reap the rewards from our efforts, with the release of Laurent's tracks Acid Eiffel (as Choice, together with Shazz) and Wake Up, as well as Lunatic Asylum's The Meltdown.

Between 1992 and 1994, we also ran a weekly party at Rex Club called Wake Up on Thursday nights. These parties offered us the opportunity to test new tracks and understand if any had the potential to turn into a success—such as the early works of Laurent and Lunatic Asylum. Consequently, an array of these tracks ended up being licensed to internationally acclaimed labels such as Transmat, Warp and Sony.

Although I signed the rights of Warp for the French territories, Fnac seemed hardly interested in electronic music at the time. Up until 1993, the label was losing money because of its limited infrastructure. This combination of factors led to us starting our own platform.

Yet, it was never my dream to start something for myself. I was earning a steady income from working for these big music companies and I also felt I gained enough support within them: it was comfortable. But when Fnac eventually got into financial trouble and as we noticed the success of the Dance Division in 1993, we felt we had to carry on. It was a very exciting period for the whole of Europe. So I left Fnac and Laurent joined me on this new adventure.

Also, all artists and external partners of Fnac moved along with us. So we had the names, the reputation and the infrastructure already in place, which made a tremendous difference as opposed to starting a label from scratch. F Communications felt like an organically developed new chapter.

Back then, electronic music wasn't labelled as house or techno on those early club nights: basically everything could be played and we were heavily influenced by that diversity. So we wanted to be very diverse as well: not house, techno or trance, but just good music. The most important question we asked ourselves was if we would buy the track at a record shop.

Around that time, everyone in France, even the journalists, seemed to hate electronic music. It was even difficult to sell the music I was licensing from abroad back then. I believed this would only change when French artists would have achieved worldwide success.

Hence, our vision was to set French artists on the map within the global music scene, after which this sound would be deemed credible within France as well. Up to that point, it proved hard for them to find a domestic home for their music. An eloquent example is St. Germain, who initially started to work with a Belgian label because there was no suitable option for him in France.

With the label, we wanted to make clear that we are French, the artists are French. It was part of the image and strategy of the label. We initially wanted to brand the label as F Records (the 'F' referring to either 'French' or 'Fuck'), but to avoid being pigeonholed as record makers only we chose to go for F Communications—which was also a nod to British label KLF Communications, ran by The KLF.

Back in 1992, Didier Lestrade—a music journalist at a newspaper called Libération—told me that if I wanted to make an impact we needed to have a visual identity making the connection with every release. That same year, a designer named Geneviève Gauckler had created unique artwork for a Fnac release. With Didier's advice in mind, we decided to stick to her line of works. She created all our designs, covers and advertisements for the next decade.

With these new responsibilities, we also had to make financial projections: according to our plan, we had to invest money for the first one year and a half before earning anything. In reality, it turned out more successful than expected and we were making profits from that first year on already. Our third release, The Milky Way by Aurora Borealis, turned out to be an enormous success and was quickly followed by the first EP from St. Germain and the first album from Laurent.

An electronic music album was something very unusual back then, as the format seemed strictly relevant for pop artists. But after a trip to the United States, Laurent told me he was bored with 12's. We discussed the idea and decided to take a shot in the dark. Even our distributor wasn't too happy with the idea, but its reception was outstanding.

Meanwhile, we were listening to every demo we received: not only from friends, but from everyone really. Many artists we signed were discovered this way, such as Aqua Bassino, A Reminiscent Drive and Jori Hulkkonen. Their profiles and backgrounds weren't important at all: it was just about the music. However, our intention has been to work with artists in the long run, something that wasn't common back then. It was a philosophy we believed in and seemed to be shared with only a few large-scale labels such as Harthouse, R&S and Warp.

Fast-forwarding some years into the new millennium, the market changed considerably—in large part because of the upcoming download culture. Laurent and I agreed, from the early days onward, to run the label for as long as we enjoyed it. Part of it was to take up big challenges, such as setting up our media network, distribution and running parties. But into this new era, there were few challenges for us to be taken.

Laurent, amongst other French artists such as Daft Punk, gained significant success with his works, which led to a big shift in the global perception of electronic music. Our main job was just to sell more records. It was all right, but didn't have the same taste. As we kept losing money between 2003 and 2006, I felt the time had come to end the project in 2007. I would have preferred to stop earlier, but you cannot halt the course of a big bus instantly.

When I discovered electronic music, I felt immediately connected to the spiritual effect of these sounds. It was a surprise, because I was raised in Africa for the first ten years of my life—as my parents were teachers there. Back then, we went to parties and listened to African music as well as American disco. I was constantly hearing strange things about shamans at my school and the mysteries of life are an important part of African culture.

Back in Paris, I discovered electronic music and its trancy effects: being on the dance floor for hours, surrounded by this cocktail of sound, lights, stroboscopes and drugs. The scene was only about three hundred or four hundred people. We would meet in the same clubs and warehouses every weekend. It felt very primitive: the repetition of the music, enhanced by substances and the DJ starring as the shaman at the helm of this tribal atmosphere. It made me happy to see all these European kids on the same wavelength, similar to what has been going on around the globe for centuries.

Trance has been present in the life of men since the dawn of time, weaving a new sense of collectivity through modified states of consciousness. The clear difference with disco or hardcore techno, to me, is that you don't feel that spiritual side so much—except maybe for a track like I Feel Love by Donna Summer, although the rhythm was very different. You generally miss the strings, the soaring melodies and the repetitive elements that capture the heart and mind. I really loved that and these experiences definitely had an influence on the label's output.

Back in the day, DJs such as Paul van Dyk and Sven Väth used to play a lot of trance, but they were not rejected by the techno scene. Unfortunately, the following waves of trance music were more cliché-prone and the productions proved imaginatively poor. For some reason its visual identity also changed entirely after 1995 and trance evolved into a wholly different scene, miles away from its initial incarnations and ideals."

Eric's favourite F Communications tracks:
A REMINISCENT DRIVE—*Life Is Beautiful*
DEEPSIDE—*Prélusion*
LAURENT GARNIER—*Acid Eiffel*

LOST LANGUAGE
Benjamin Woods
28 April 1980, Peterborough, United Kingdom

"I grew up mostly listening to guitar music and playing in bands, but my first encounter with electronic music came on a family holiday to Mallorca, when an older lad I made friends with gave me a cassette recording of Lifeforms by The Future Sound Of London.

I was about fourteen years old and that dark, electronic, sci-fi atmosphere really hit me. The Prodigy, Leftfield and the likes were already on my radar, thanks to the alternative music press and local indie discos, but The Future Sound Of London opened me up to bands like The Orb and Orbital, two of the big festival acts at the time, who were similarly exploring more techno and electronica sounds.

Not long after—it must have been around 1996 or 1997, I got a job in a local record store called Our Price, which morphed into one of the first Virgin Megastores. Everything was 'mega-sized' in the business back then, especially dance music compilations. I used to spend my money on Goa-directed mix CDs, eventually finding my way to the Reactivate series, where I first heard Humate's Love Stimulation. That was a big moment.

The Renaissance series was a huge influence too, especially the Ian Ossia/Nigel Dawson compilation that came out in 1998. There was an eerie, wistful melancholy in these strange, dark melodies that I really connected with. Musical parallels could be made with bands like Joy Division, The Smiths and The Cure. And then the superclub thing started to blow up and that whole sound translated perfectly to big events.

I moved to London in early 1999 to work at Pinnacle Distribution and started hanging out at The Gallery, where I met some Gatecrasher regulars. I was soon travelling up to Sheffield for Gatecrasher every week. The night would typically start with slower, techier house tracks, building up to the faster, riffier trance tunes. Tracks like Hardy Heller's I.C.E. 794 created a perfect bridge between these different genres. Matt Hardwick dropped it just before midnight on my first visit to Gatecrasher and you could just feel the shift.

    I received a lot of vinyl promos whilst working for Pinnacle, which became currency when swapping them with A&R guys at the record labels I liked. I used to swap a lot of the west coast deep house vinyl I received with Sean from Hooj Choons, who eventually asked me to join them in a junior A&R position sometime around late summer 1999. I absolutely loved that label, so this really was a dream come true.

At that time, Hooj was moving into deeper, more tech-driven territories with artists such as Killahurtz, Morel and Silvio Ecomo and they needed a suitable home for their trance output—which is how Lost Language was born. I was known as the 'trance guy' so they let me take the reins. I was really proud that Sean and Jerry at Hooj trusted me to lead Lost Language so soon after joining and at such a young age. Jerry referred to me as Ben Lost in an interview and it stuck.

Some big names such as Tilt, Solarstone and Lustral had found their home at Hooj over the years, so we often got first refusal on any new material they had written. We also signed tracks from various European labels such as Lightning and Black Hole, back when territorial rights meant something and we'd then commission our own remixes. In those days, a lot of time was spent trawling through demos that had been sent in on CDR, sorting them into 'yes', 'maybe' and 'no' piles. The 'no' pile was a bin.

A stand out release for me in the early days and one that sort of kickstarted my DJ career as Ben Lost, was Solarstone's Solarcoaster. I remember looking through the DATs on our massive shelf of masters and coming across an old demo of unfinished Solarstone tracks and ideas. I stuck it on and couldn't believe it had been sitting there gathering dust when that massive True Romance [movie by Quentin Tarantino from 1993] sample dropped.

I sent a copy straight to DJ Tiësto, who was a big fan of the label and was in the middle of compiling his third In Search Of Sunrise compilation. Solarcoaster had this Balearic riff that I knew he'd love and would totally fit the ethos of that series. He worked it into the album last minute and I got a special thanks in the credits. I was a massive fan of Tiësto and that series, so I was really proud to have played a small part in shaping that mix.

I'm not sure what made us different from other labels, though. There was just so much quality around at that time. Like our peers, such as Bonzai and Platipus, we had a deep understanding of a particular sound. Fans of the label said they trusted us and could buy our releases blind, knowing the quality would be there. And when things started to get a little more 'Euro', Lost Language stuck with a more progressive outlook.

In homage to the way Hooj operated, we happily commissioned ambient, house and breaks remixes. That was something we were always open to. Our artwork was also relatively clean and classy and again like Hooj, there was a recurring theme that seemed to appeal.

Twelve-inch singles were big business in the late nineties and early noughties and we'd receive compilation licensing requests on an almost daily basis, so when that side of the business started to crumble in 2003, with downloads and CDJs becoming the norm, we knew the genie was out of the bottle and there was probably no going back.

We tried a few things to keep the fire burning and felt that if we got a 'hit' we would be able to weather the storm a little longer. With trance still a huge commercial enterprise, we felt Lost Language was our best bet. Having had some success with Armin Van Buuren's remix of Seven Cities in 2002, we stuck out a white label of Marco V's remix of Café Del Mar, the first few of which simply had Café Del Mar scrawled on them in marker pen to add a bit of mystery. It went on to have some decent radio support and was a big festival tune in the summer of 2003. I heard it played four times at Homelands.

We had a further few last-minute commercial rolls of the dice, one of which was a vocal abomination that I'm not at all proud of having in our back catalogue. We had to try though, with jobs and mortgages at stake. It nearly worked. New management came in and I eventually left the label around 2004 or 2005, to concentrate on some other (ultimately doomed) musical pursuits, before returning in 2012—in what Mixmag referred to as 'the sabbatical to end all sabbaticals'.

It's a very different scene now. Music has become so much more accessible, which is surely positive. I still love good trance—simple, hypnotic, melodic. It's great hearing more of that in the current techno scene. Trance had a bad reputation, but history has been kind in recent years. There's not a lot worse than 'bad trance', but who am I to determine what that is? DJ Laurent invented trance, mixing goth, acid house and Belgian new beat on tape decks in

Goa back in the late eighties and he probably has something to say about the late nineties trance scene I was involved in, so it's all relative."

Benjamin's favourite Lost Language tracks:
ACCADIA—*Into The Dawn*
LYRIC & NATALI—*Over Emotion*
ROLAND KLINKENBERG—*Inner Laugh*

MASTERMINDED FOR SUCCESS
Mark Reeder
5 January 1958, Manchester, United Kingdom

"In the last months of 1989, just prior to the fall of the Berlin wall, I had been invited by the Amiga—the state-owned record label of East Germany—to produce an album in East Berlin, by an East German indie band called Die Vision. This album called Torture consequently became the last album of communist German Democratic Republic.

In the process of making this album, I encountered the top level of Amiga's management and A&R. After the fall of the wall, they rushed to change the label name to ZONG and I saw this as an opportunity for them to move forward musically, now that all the restraints of the communist regime had fallen away. Finally they could release new kinds of music they had otherwise not been able to even consider under the communists.

Optimistically, I suggested they release a great new style of dance music that I had been listening to in the UFO club in West Berlin and we called techno. I imagined there would be lots of young, untapped talent scattered around East Germany and these kids would also need a label. This change would provide the perfect opportunity. I also knew that most western record labels and especially the major labels, wouldn't give these kids the time of day, let alone sign them. So I thought, if we can provide them with a platform, then we can nurture and guide them.

Unfortunately, the ex-Amiga heads had never even heard of techno (in fact, they didn't even know what a twelve-inch single was, as all DJs in the German Democratic Republic played from cassette tapes). So after a couple of months of frustration and much attempted persuasion, they suggested that I should do a label myself and offered me the use of their infrastructure and pressing facilities.

I occupied their demo-listening room 101, which was Hermann Göring's former office overlooking the Reichstag, and thought about giving my label a name. I really wanted to use the letters MFS (the abbreviation of the STASI, the East German secret police) as it was constantly in the news at that time and I thought it would shock and probably terrorise many of the parents of all the 'Eastie' kids buying my records. I also knew that it was a sensitive subject and that the ex-Amiga people would never agree to do it.

Therefore, I needed a good cover for the initials. Sitting with my friend Dave Rimmer, we doodled around working out possible names that could mask these initials. We laughed at stupid ideas like Martians From Space, More Fucking Sex or Megacity Future Sounds. I wanted Success in the name and Dave suggested Mastermind. Thus the name Masterminded for Success was born. I also needed to find some 'Eastie' artists for my 'Eastie' label. I thought now the wall had come down, these kids would all be rushing out to buy Atari computers and making music, but that sadly wasn't the case.

East Germany had only recently been incorporated into the Federal Republic of Germany and computers were still expensive. Even if there were talented people out there, most of them didn't even realise it at that stage. I needed to act and was forced to turn to some of my music friends in West Berlin. The first signing was a project called Effective Force. Their music wasn't even dance music, although it was electronic and quite cinematic.

    I also had the ex-Amiga lot breathing down my neck. They decided that, as they were going to initially pay for the pressings, they also wanted to have a say on what I could release. I knew it was hopeless to fight them if I wanted to make anything of my label. They knew absolutely nothing about dance music and even less about techno, yet I knew it would be the only way to move forward. So I swallowed my pride and allowed them to choose two tracks from a pile of dreadful demos. I also knew that they would soon lose interest and I would eventually be allowed to just get on with it. Which is exactly what happened!

One afternoon, they proudly announced that they had closed the distribution arm of the ex-Amiga. This was a major blow. Instead of offering East German distribution to western labels, they had closed their distribution. I couldn't believe it. If there was one thing that was valuable to them, it was their distribution network. They knew where every record shop was in the former German Democratic Republic, and now it was gone. This also meant I would have to find a new distributor.

I had a couple of releases ready to go, but no distributor. I approached Jürgen Laarmann, who was running a small fanzine called Frontpage, and I explained to him that Amiga had given me a marketing budget and I could place regular ads in his mag, but only if he could help me find a distributor. The next day I had one.

It was also around this time that I realised that most of my British friends were having difficulty in connecting with this new sound of techno. They were all still listening to rave bands such as Happy Mondays, Inspiral Carpets or Stone Roses and had no real idea about the musical revolution that was happening in Germany. I thought about what it was that was missing for them. What could I give them to help them to connect to this new electronic dance sound? It was a hookline. They needed some form of a melody or hook to go along with the pounding beats.

Being a regular clubber myself, I also knew that emotional feeling of euphoria everyone got to absorb as it rippled through a club while everyone was dancing to the same tune on E. How would it be possible to harness this emotion and combine it with music? I wanted to take the emotional upheaval caused by the fall of the wall (and Germany's consequent reunification), the elation of winning the world cup and mix it all with the emotional ups and downs induced by ecstasy, combining it with hypnotic, trance-inducing sequencers, like a mixture of Tangerine Dream and Mahler or Wagner-like chord changes, all held together by a driving drum machine. This music I initially called hypno-trance.

Around that time, I had a meeting with Harald Blüchel, a young musician friend, who I knew was looking for a new label. I told him about my idea and asked whether he would be willing to try and interpret it musically. Being classically trained I thought he'd understand the mixture of melody and hypnotic rhythm I was after.

I released his Transcendental Overdrive EP and we relabelled his sound MFS trance-dance. This was eventually shortened in Frontpage, to be simply known as trance. I released other trance tracks by Mijk van Dijk (as Mindgear), GTO and Neutron9000 before releasing the first trance compilation called Tranceformed From Beyond. I asked Harald and Mijk to remix and sequence the tracks together like a DJ mix to enhance the trance-inducing effect on the listener.

When I started MFS in 1990, there was no such thing as a global trance market. It didn't exist. Even techno was still a niche. I mainly wanted to provide a platform for young Eastern European artists. I was open to anyone really, as long as they had something interesting to offer. All changed once I started to release trance records on MFS.

The first successful record was The Visions Of Shiva's Perfect Day. It was a collaboration between Harald and a young DJ he'd met at a Dubmission party called Paul van Dyk. Everyone had loved Harald's first MFS release as Cosmic Baby, but the DJs were having problems playing it in clubs, as it was not DJ-friendly.

> "I also knew that emotional feeling of euphoria everyone got to absorb as it rippled through a club while everyone was dancing to the same tune on E."

I had suggested Harald that he works with a DJ to find out what a techno DJ needs. Paul seemed to be the right person to work with at the time. Even though he didn't have the faintest idea how to make music, he did understand what a DJ requires.

To make any kind of impact internationally, it was still important back then to get some kind of recognition in the UK media and there were a handful of useful magazines that were dedicated to dance music, such as Mixmag and DJ Mag. When they gave The Visions Of Shiva a glowing review, it certainly made a huge difference and attracted a lot of attention to the label and my previous releases too.

The main reason for our success was the music. Did I like it? Would I buy it? Or did it make sense to release a track, even though I knew it wasn't perfect, but I felt the artist had immense potential—and only by releasing their first track, would it motivate them to evolve? Yes, I did that too.

I would listen to all the demo tapes we were sent. It needed to captivate me in some way: not once, not twice, but often. I feel music is very subjective: one day you might not like something because of your mood or surroundings, but the next day you listen to it with different ears and it will open up to you.

I trusted the artists to be their own quality controllers too. After all, it was their name on the record. The geographical location simply added to the mystique and obviously the image I wanted to create with the label played a role too, which incidentally was not purely as a trance label. I wanted MFS to be an electronic music label for all genres.

Of course, when a record goes through the roof, the artist involved becomes the focal point and this could cause all kinds of accusations. Fact is, as a label we needed at least one successful artist so that we could support the less successful ones until they were ready. I always tried to treat every MFS artist equally whenever it was possible. It's just a coincidence that we became known for trance, due to the international success of Paul van Dyk.

One of my most vivid memories was after The Visions Of Shiva split, when Paul concentrated on remix work and his first mix compilation, the MFS and K7 audio/video collaboration X-Mix 1—The MFS Trip. Paul wanted this mix album to be his best work to date. We borrowed a four-track reel-to-reel tape deck and he spent the whole day recording the mix and making little over-dubs, effects, etcetera.

The master tape was due to be collected at ten PM that night, for use on the X-Mix 1 video soundtrack. I arrived at Paul's flat just as he was mixing in the last track. He was very excited and so happy with his work. Once the outro was completed, Paul immediately hit the rewind button so I could hear the entire piece and we sat down to relax.

The tape deck swished into action and smoothly started to gain speed and rewind the tape, building up and up to a whirlwind speed. Suddenly there was a malfunction and the tape deck started spinning completely out of control. It spewed all the tape out, stretched it and mashed it up, as the tape wound itself tight around the reels, eventually snapping it and that all before Paul had managed to leap up and stop the machine. The tape was ruined and very obviously beyond repair. Paul threw himself onto his bed in tears. He only had about an hour to go before the courier arrives to collect the master.

Thankfully, I managed to encourage him to start again. So wasting no time, I salvaged as much tape I could off the reel and he set to work, basically trying to reconstruct his mix from memory. He had to start from the very beginning. I helped him with the effects and some track selection. This mix is, therefore, absolutely live-as-it-happened sixty minutes with no overdubs or edits, as he finished it literally moments before the courier arrived to collect it.

By 1999 I had certainly become bored of what was being marketed as trance. It was like music-by-numbers. The same sampled kick drum, the same synth string sound, the same breakdown with a massive drum roll. It was becoming a parody of itself. It was tedious and had nothing to do with trance. It didn't even induce a trance-like state: Berlin dub masters Basic Channel were in that sense more trancy.

Musically, I felt restricted by the fact that MFS was being known only as a trance label. I wanted to move in a different direction and design something different for the coming new millennium. That's why I created Wet & Hard with Corvin Dalek. It was a dance derivative, sexual and groovy. After Corvin decided to hang up his headphones in 2007, I quit MFS and got back into production and making music myself.

The trance of today is actually nothing like I had initially imagined it. It certainly coloured the image of my label though. How it will be viewed in the future in the realm of electronic music is hard for me to predict, so I won't, but I think it will most probably be up there with EDM. It has had its place and for a time it was fashionable. It's quite a nice feeling, being a part of that achievement. It was a much yearned for counter-balance to the techno movement and the cheesier and cheaper trance became, the more intellectual it made techno appear."

Mark's favourite MFS tracks:
COSMIC BABY—*Stellar Supreme*
PAUL VAN DYK—*Seven Ways*
VARIOUS—*Tranceformed From Beyond*

Tiësto In Concert, 2003 © Rutger Geerling/ID&T

"The only real impact 'trance' in this context has had on wider musical culture is a legacy of overdriven, hollow commerciality, endlessly repeated and commodified, until it's just a bunch of post-EDM noise, topped off by sh*t 'pop stars', dripping out of crap radio stations or as a backdrop for depressing, selfie-driven festivals."

RED JERRY, HOOJ CHOONS

Johan Gielen at Trance Energy, 2004 © Rutger Geerling/ID&T

Rank 1 at Trance Energy, 2004 © Rutger Geerling/ID&T

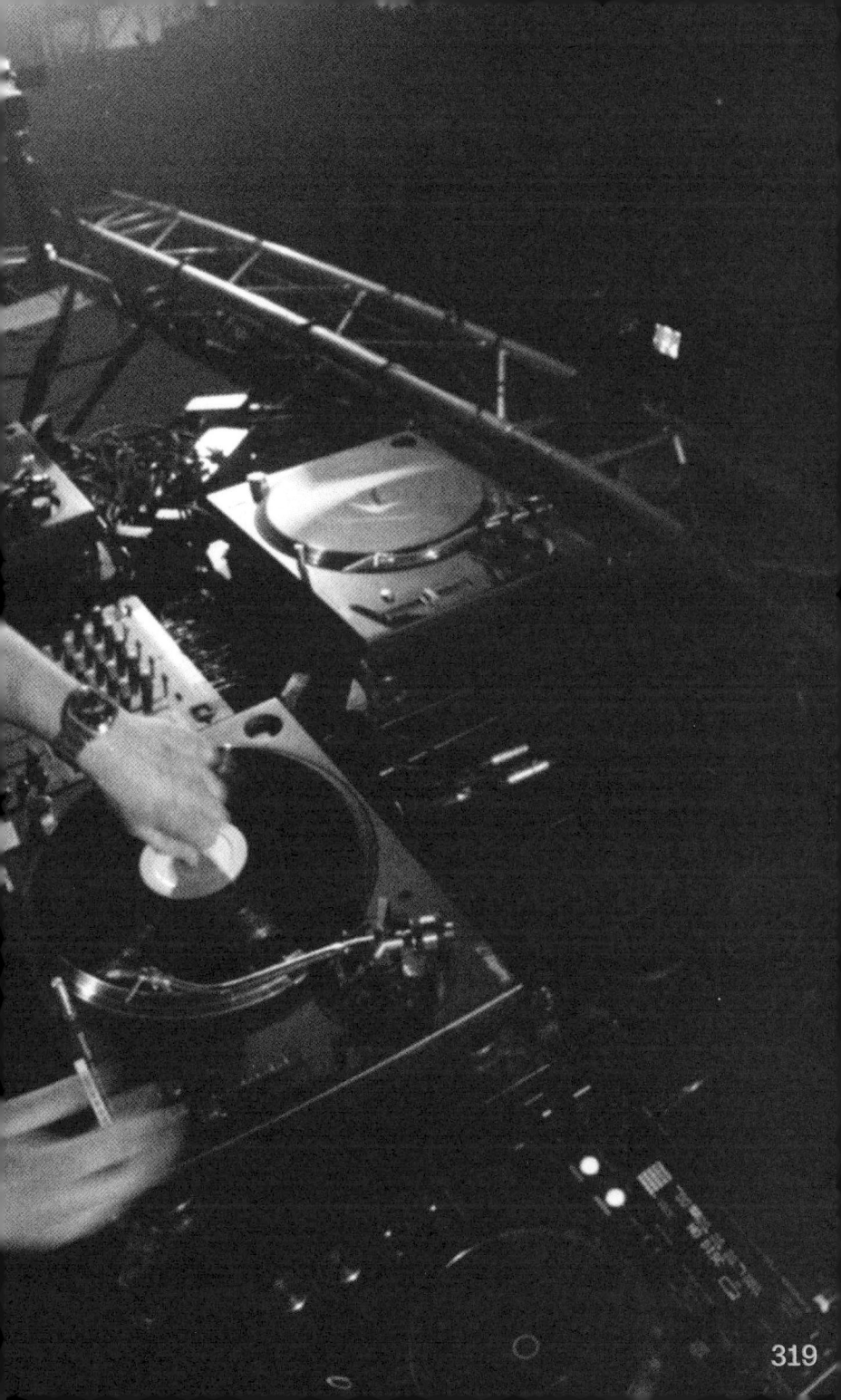

ALBUMS

Aside from the popularity of the 12" single format in trance music, compact discs became the standard format to reach the commercial market during the nineties. CDs were relatively small, lightweight, easy to store and stable in terms of audio quality. With its extended playtime of up to eighty minutes, the CD format also offered more playtime compared to a single vinyl record.

Synchronous with the popularity of the format, technological inventions such as portable devices and CD players in cars made listening to one's favourite music now possible for everyone and everywhere. The availability of CDs was another major leap in the format's success: whereas vinyls were mostly limited to being stocked in record stores, the relatively small storage size of CDs made their way into alternative outlets such as supermarkets, gas stations and book stores.

The CD format enabled artists to experiment with new artistic approaches in the form of full-length albums. Album projects were capable of showcasing an artistic vision, a palette of sounds wider than the one-off club-directed record. Artist albums, more so than singles, offer the benefit of extensive duration, providing the artist with more time to tell their story and cover different musical grounds.

Aside from albums, mix compilations proved to be a catalyst for showcasing trance artists to a wider extent. Compilation projects generally required more processing to match tracks coming from various sources and labels. When it comes to trance mixes, an additional challenge comes with mixing different records together in order to create a single flow out of contrasting cuts and arrangements, similar to that of what one could experience in the club.

This section features twenty-five artist albums that were not necessarily successful in a commercial sense, but were able to widen the spectrum of trance music in one way or another. These albums are either hallmarks of the original sound, explored new musical territories, reached new audiences, or accidentally found their way under the trance banner. It is safe to say that many of these artists did not intend to create an album that would be coined trance music. More importantly, these artists did want to capture the feeling and mood that became so closely associated with the term.

The label, catalogue, country and year tags generally refer to the first official CD pressing of the release. Mix versions are only mentioned when different versions or (re)mixes are available on the stated release. Outlining a broad range of artists and titles, only one release per alias is featured in order to keep the selection varied.

A

ART OF TRANCE
—Wildlife On One
Label	Platipus
Catalogue	PLAT25CD
Country	United Kingdom
Year	1996
01.	Kaleidoscope
02.	Mosquito
03.	Gloria (Transparent Mix)
04.	Haagen Daaz
05.	Octopus (Original Mix)
06.	Golden Rain
07.	Deeper Than Deep
08.	Blue Owl
09.	Emerald Eyes
10.	Cambodia (Tunnel Vision Mix)

ASTRAL PROJECTION
—Trust In Trance
Label	Phonokol
Catalogue	2041-2
Country	Israel
Year	1996
01.	Kabalah
02.	Enlightened Evolution
03.	The Feelings
04.	Utopia
05.	Black & White
06.	People Can Fly
07.	Radial Blur
08.	Aurora Borealis
09.	Still Dreaming (Anything Can Happen)

ATB
—Movin' Melodies
Label	Kontor Records
Catalogue	KONTOR068
Country	Germany
Year	1999
01.	The First Tones
02.	Emotion
03.	Underwater World
04.	Zwischenstück
05.	9 PM (Till I Come)
06.	Killer 2000
07.	Too Much Rain (ATB vs. Woody van Eyden United Deejays For Central America Mix)
08.	Don't Stop
09.	Obsession
10.	My Dream
11.	Kayama
12.	Beach Vibes
13.	Movin' Melodies
14.	Sunburn
15.	9 PM (Till I Come) (Signum Mix)

B

BLUE PLANET CORPORATION
—Blue Planet
Label	Flying Rhino Records
Catalogue	AFRCD17
Country	United Kingdom
Year	1999
01.	Apex
02.	Crystal
03.	Alidade
04.	Micromega
05.	Atoll
06.	Dialect
07.	Open Sea
08.	Roma
09.	Arcana

BT
—Movement In Still Life
Label	Headspace
Catalogue	HEDSCDA001
Country	United Kingdom
Year	1999
01.	Movement In Still Life
02.	Ride
03.	Madskillz —Mic Chekka
04.	The Hip Hop Phenomenon
05.	Mercury And Solace
06.	Dreaming
07.	Giving Up The Ghost
08.	Godspeed
09.	Namistai
10.	Running Down The Way Up
11.	Satellite

C

CHICANE
—Behind The Sun
Label	Xtravaganza Recordings
Catalogue	XTRAV10CD
Country	United Kingdom
Year	2000
01.	Overture
02.	Low Sun
03.	No Ordinary Morning
04.	Saltwater (Original)
05.	Halcyon
06.	Autumn Tactics
07.	Overlap
08.	Don't Give Up
09.	Saltwater (The Thrillseekers Remix)
10.	Andromeda

COSMIC BABY
—Stellar Supreme
Label	MFS
Catalogue	MFS7033-2
Country	Germany
Year	1992
01.	The Space Track
02.	Stimme Der Energie
03.	Stellar Supreme
04.	Heaven's Tears
05.	Planet Earth 1993 (Blue)
06.	The Pianotrack (Yellow)
07.	Sea Of Tranquility

08. Cosmic Trigger 5.1.
09. Sweet Dreams For Kaa - My Love
10. Studio Or Spaceship
11. Galaxia
12. Cosmic Force
13. Eurovoodoo
14. Liebe (Red)
15. The Universal Mind

DJ TIËSTO
—*In My Memory*
Label: Magik Muzik
Catalogue: MAGIKMUZIKCD01
Country: Netherlands
Year: 2001
01. Magik Journey
02. Close To You
03. Dallas 4 PM
04. In My Memory
05. Obsession
06. Battleship Grey
07. Flight 643
08. Lethal Industry
09. Suburban Train

EARTH NATION
—*Terra Incognita*
Label: Eye Q Records
Catalogue: 063011674-2
Country: Germany
Year: 1995
01. Way In
02. First Interlude
03. Transfiguration
04. Elucidate
05. The Ikarus Syndrome
06. Second Interlude
07. An Artificial Dream
08. Last Interlude
09. Outburst
10. Green Sky Is Red
11. Mentality

KAITO
—*Special Life*
Label: Kompakt
Catalogue: KOMPAKTCD19
Country: Germany
Year: 2002
01. Release Your Body
02. Air Rider
03. Inside River
04. Intension
05. Saturday And Sunday
06. Breaking The Star
07. Everlasting
08. Scene
09. Respect To The Distance
10. Awakening (Beatlesstrumental)

L.S.G.
—*Rendezvous In Outer Space*
Label: Superstition
Catalogue: SUPERSTITION2038CD
Country: Germany
Year: 1995
01. Wrong Time... Wrong Place
02. Lonely Casseopaya
03. My Time Is Yours
04. Can You See The Yellow Turtles
05. Miss Understanding
06. Sweet Gravity
07. Sweet G (#2)
08. The Hidden Sun Of Venus
09. Lunar Orbit
10. Everything Is...
11. Enter - Paradise
12. Fontana
13. Reprise

MAN WITH NO NAME
—*Moment Of Truth*
Label: Concept In Dance
Catalogue: DICCD125
Country: United Kingdom
Year: 1996
01. Moment Of Truth
02. Floor-Essence (Dayglo Mix)
03. Subterfuge
04. Evolution
05. Azymuth
06. Low Commotion
07. Skydiving
08. Dawn Chorus
09. Cairo
10. Sugar Rush (Refined Mix)
11. Cosmic Echoes

MAURO PICOTTO
—*The Album*
Label: Zeitgeist
Catalogue: 549-224-2
Country: Germany
Year: 2000
01. Lounge
02. Pulsar
03. Komodo
04. Like This Like That
05. Bug
06. Planet
07. Proximus Medley With Adiemus
08. Lizard
09. Ultimahora Ibiza
10. Iguana
11. Eclectic
12. Underground
13. Pegasus
14. Baguette

OM
—*Instant Enlightenment*

(Deep Trance Ambient Experience)
Label   C&S Records
Catalogue   CS8513
Country   United States
Year   1993
01. Seed Of Sound
02. Wheels Of Light
03. Here Comes The Sun
04. Human Love
05. Physical Reality
06. Virtual High
07. Are You Experienced?
08. Peace Of Mind
09. Be Here Now
10. Big Chill Out II
11. Ectoplasm

PAUL OAKENFOLD
—Bunkka
Label   Perfecto
Catalogue   PERFALB09CD
Country   United Kingdom
Year   2002
01. Ready Steady Go
02. Southern Sun
03. Time Of Your Life
04. Hypnotised
05. Zoo York
06. Nixon's Spirit
07. Hold Your Hand
08. Starry Eyed Surprise
09. Get Em Up
10. Motion
11. The Harder They Come

PAUL VAN DYK
—45 RPM
Label   MFS
Catalogue   MFS7066-2
Country   Germany
Year   1994
01. Introjection
02. I'm Comin' (To Take You Away)
03. For An Angel
04. 45 RPM
05. Spannung (Tension)
06. Emergency!
07. Rushin' (Revolutions Per Minute)
08. Pump This Party (Video Edit)
09. Ooh! La! La! (Krankenhouse Mix)
10. A Magical Moment
11. Pump This 45
12. Ejaculoutro

PUSH
—From Beyond
Label   Lightning Records
Catalogue   1-00-27
Country   Belgium
Year   2000
01. Electro Fever
02. Universal Nation
03. Strange World
04. Travelogue
05. Cosmonautica
06. Till We Meet Again...
07. Tranzy State Of Mind
08. The Legacy
09. Live On
10. Outro

RANK 1
—Symsonic
Label   ID&T
Catalogue   7004502
Country   Netherlands
Year   2002
01. Symsonic
02. Cosmomatic
03. Airwave (Album Cut)
04. Conspiracy
05. T.T.C.
06. Awakening (Radio Edit)
07. Down From The Deep
08. Equilibrium
09. Such Is Life (Sunday Afternoon Rework)
10. Passage To The Unknown
11. Still In My Mind
12. Airwave (Sunset Mix)
13. Such Is Life (Album Cut)
14. The Citrus Juicer

ROBERT LEINER
—Visions Of The Past
Label   Apollo
Catalogue   AMB3925CD
Country   Belgium
Year   1994
01. Out Of Control
02. Visions Of The Past
03. Interval
04. To Places You've Never Been
05. Aqua Viva
06. Full Moon Ritual
07. Zenit
08. Dream Or Reality
09. From Beyond And Back
10. Northern Dark

ROBERT MILES
—Dreamland
Label   DBX Records
Catalogue   DBX030CD
Country   Italy
Year   1996
01. Children (Dream Version)
02. Fable (Message Version)
03. Fantasya
04. Landscape
05. In My Dreams
06. Princess Of Light
07. Fable (Dream Version)
08. In The Dawn
09. Children (Original Version)
10. Red Zone

SVEN VÄTH

—Accident In Paradise

Label	Eye Q Records
Catalogue	4509-91193-2
Country	Germany
Year	1992
01.	Ritual Of Life
02.	Caravan Of Emotions
03.	L'esperanca
04.	Sleeping Invention
05.	Mellow Illusion
06.	Merry-Go-Round Somewhere
07.	An Accident In Paradise
08.	Drifting Like Whales In The Darkness
09.	Coda

SYSTEM F
—Out Of The Blue

Label	Tsunami
Catalogue	TSU1504
Country	Netherlands
Year	2001
01.	Lost In Motion
02.	Indian Summer
03.	Out Of The Blue
04.	Elevate
05.	Insolation
06.	Cry
07.	Needlejuice
08.	Soul On Soul
09.	Exhale
10.	Solstice
11.	Mode Confusion
12.	Cry (Unplugged)

THE FUTURE SOUND OF LONDON
—Lifeforms

Label	Virgin
Catalogue	CDV2722
Country	United Kingdom
Year	1994
CD1	
01.	Cascade
02.	Ill Flower
03.	Flak
04.	Bird Wings
05.	Dead Skin Cells
06.	Lifeforms
07.	Eggshell
08.	Among Myselves
CD2	
01.	Domain
02.	Spineless Jelly
03.	Interstat
04.	Vertical Pig
05.	Cerebral
06.	Life Form Ends
07.	Vit
08.	Omnipresence
09.	Room 208
10.	Elaborate Burn
11.	Little Brother

UNIONJACK
—There Will Be No Armageddon

Label	Platipus
Catalogue	PLAT15CD
Country	United Kingdom
Year	1995
01.	Red Herring
02.	Cactus
03.	Water Drums
04.	Two Full Moons And A Trout (14" Mix)
05.	No Life Can Survive Here
06.	Frornage Frais
07.	Lollipop Man
08.	There Will Be No Armageddon
09.	Toucan
10.	Epilogue

YOUNG AMERICAN PRIMITIVE
—Young American Primitive

Label	ZoëMagik Records
Catalogue	ZM-CD001
Country	United States
Year	1993
01.	Intro
02.	Trance Formation
03.	Flux
04.	Young American Primitive
05.	Ritual
06.	Sunrise
07.	Daydream
08.	Over And Out
09.	These Waves
10.	Monolith Part One
11.	Monolith Part Two

Trance Energy, 2005 © Rutger Geerling/ID&T

DISCLAIMER

No part of this publication may be reproduced or utilised in any form or by any means, mechanical or electronic, including, but not limited to, photo-copying, scanning and recording by any information and retrieval system, without written consent from the publisher.

All views and opinions expressed in this publication are solely those of the author and the people being interviewed. These views do not necessarily represent those of the publisher.

Photographic material and artwork in this publication have been reproduced with permission of the copyright holders as much as possible. Untraced copyright holders should contact the publisher, also with regard to unintended omissions and/or attribution errors.

ACKNOWLEDGEMENTS

I am deeply grateful for the trust and efforts of Arne van Terphoven, Arny Bink, Baptiste Girou, François Maas, Luc Kheradmand, Nader Mirebrahimi, Pim Warnars, Rosanne Janmaat, Rutger Geerling, Ryan Griffin, Sébastien Robert and especially Thomas Hervé in making this project happen. My sincere gratitude also goes out to all artists and label managers who were willing to share their personal stories.

REFERENCES

I made use of the following sources to develop this book: Bleep43, Crack Magazine, Discogs, DJ Mag, Dummy Mag, Dutch Dance, Electronic Beats, Fact Magazine, ID&T, Mary Go Wild, Pitchfork, Red Bull Music Academy, Resident Advisor, The Guardian, Thump, Wikipedia and YouTube.

COLOPHON

Author	Arjan Rietveld
Design	Thomas Hervé
	hervethomas.com
Editorial	Baptiste Girou
Photography	Pim Warnars
	Rutger Geerling
	ID&T
Partners	Black Hole Recordings
	Field Records
Publishing	Perfect Wave
ISBN	978-90-820758-9-2

Copyright © Arjan Rietveld
First published in 2021
Fourth edition, 2025
Manufactured in Lithuania

hypnotised.nl